Golf Positive! Live Positive!

Golf Positive! Live Positive!

Lessons in golf and life

Debbie O'Connell

ISBN-13: 9781533148360
ISBN-10: 1533148368

Library of Congress Control Number: 2016907781
CreateSpace Independent Publishing Platform
North Charleston, South Carolina

Contents

Acknowledgements

Thank you to my partner in life, my best friend, my wife, Jennifer. Her constant support, endless belief and ongoing encouragement is the reason this book became a reality! I'm so thankful for our amazing "kids" - Mickey (our dog) and Noodle (our cat) - who sat with me and comforted me throughout this endeavor. I treasure the many miles Mickey and I have shared to keep my energy and spirits high!

Thank you to mom and dad for being my pillars of love and strength for my entire life! My family has always offered a source of inspiration. They call me crazy, sometimes, but "In a good way!"

My coach Lisa Toste guided, motivated, challenged and stretched me throughout the entire process of writing this book. Thank you so much for sharing your wisdom and encouraging me to make all of my dreams come true!

Thank you to those who provided their expertise in reviewing the content and editing this presentation!

To the LPGA organization and my fellow LPGA Professionals: You are my coaches and mentors ... thank you! I value all that you have taught me and look forward to my continued education and growth.

Thank you to all those who are always striving to golf positive and live positive. You inspire me!

Introduction

Learned much from the lesson tee and seek to share it with golfers and non-golfers alike. Life has its victories, hazards, celebrations, bunkers, sunny days, and storms—just like golf.

Golf is certainly a metaphor for life. For many years, I have studied and taught the game of golf as well as personal development and success strategies. My lessons involve playing the role of a psychologist to help students create breakthroughs, and sometimes acting like a bartender and just listening.

Throughout this book, you will gain knowledge and strategies to improve all areas of your golf game. In my teaching, I do not rely on a single method because one type of swing does not fit all golfers. There are basic fundamentals that will apply to most golfers, and that is my area of focus.

I will then relate each golf lesson to a life lesson. My psychology studies in college aligned perfectly with my interest in understanding people. Since I was a teenager, I have been captivated by success strategies, personal growth and continuous learning as I strive to reach my full potential in life. I have had many coaches along the way, and learned through classes, seminars, books, cassette tapes, audiobooks, videos, and movies. The totality of my education, combined with personal experiences, brings me to this point in life when I can share my knowledge with you.

In each chapter of this book, I will take you through a proven four-step strategy for success called CORE Triumph!™ The acronym CORE stands for: Coach, Outcome, Reasons, and Execution. I use the word "Triumph" to remind you to analyze your progress and maybe "tri" something different, if needed. The exclamation mark at the end means to celebrate your success!

For example, Professional Golf Association (PGA) Tour professional Jordan Spieth has been working with his *coach*, Cameron McCormick, since he was a junior player. Jordan also works with a fitness expert. His first big goal or *outcome* was to qualify for the PGA Tour. Although he failed in the second stage of Q-School in 2012 (the qualifying tournaments to earn your way onto the PGA Tour), Jordan adjusted his *execution* plan and found another way to play on the PGA Tour. He earned temporary-member status on the Tour by taking full advantage of his opportunities with sponsor exemptions. He shared with the media that one of his goals as a junior was to win the Masters, and his ultimate goal was to join (now-fellow) professional Bubba Watson as a two-time champion. Jordan achieved his initial goals, and proceeded to reset and think bigger. He doesn't always share his goals publicly, but he is always clear on his desired outcome.

Jordan has many compelling *reasons* to strive to be the best, but one that reaches into his heart is his special-needs sister, Ellie, who is seven years younger than Jordan and his biggest fan. Jordan has an *execution* plan for success and works very hard on his golf game, his physical body, and his mental focus. He also adjusts his execution plan when needed. There it is—a perfect example of CORE Triumph!

The CORE Triumph! strategy is used by almost every successful person, although it's not always labeled as such. Most successful people have mentors, know with clarity what they want to achieve, are motivated by compelling reasons, and create and execute a plan to accomplish their goals.

Successful people will also review and analyze whether their plans are working. If not, they do not give up; they try (or, for my purposes, "tri") something different. That is what I call CORE Triumph!

Repetition and taking action are keys to learning. These attributes are used in teaching both golf skills and life skills. Repeating an action turns it into a habit. A powerful habit is to use CORE Triumph! daily, which is the reason you'll see a list of coaches, outcomes, reasons, and executions near the beginning of each chapter.

I invite you to take this journey with me to explore and improve your golf game and your life. Let's reach your potential!

My Gift to You!

Y ou inspire me because of your desire to take your golf game and your life to another level. Your commitment to live a positive life was revealed when you took the time to open this book.

My vision and mission is to make a positive and powerful impact on the world. I want to empower and educate as many people as possible on how to live a happy fulfilling life. It's a calling I have felt deep inside since I was a teenager. You are now part of my mission! Let's change the world together!

Because you have made a commitment to read this book, I want to give you a gift. This gift will take the lessons you'll learn in this book to a deeper level.

My gift will reveal to you the five must have techniques to live triumphantly! Go to LivePositiveGift.com for your gift of a lifetime.

One

CORE Triumph!™: Start Your
Four-Step Plan to Success

*Our goals can only be reached through a vehicle of a plan,
in which we must fervently believe, and upon which we
must vigorously act. There is no other route to success.*

—Pablo Picasso

In this chapter, you will learn a proven four-step plan for success: CORE Triumph!™. We will examine your goals, analyze your motivations, set a plan, and get you on the path to reach your full potential. Asking quality questions will aid in creating the blueprint for success and keep you moving toward your ultimate outcome. Below, you will find the CORE Triumph! plan for this chapter.

Coaches	Outcome	Reasons	Execution
• Debbie O'Connell	• Learn, understand, and implement the success strategy	• Confidence	• Read this chapter
• Joe Matson		• The joy of success	• Work through this chapter
	• Achieve goals	• Growth	• Ask quality questions
		• A happy fulfilling life	• Answer the questions in this chapter
			• Get a coach
			• Visualize a clear outcome
			• Identify compelling reasons to achieve goal

Joe Matson was only six years old when he went to work. He was shining shoes for twenty-five cents a pair in downtown Charleston, West Virginia. "We were very poor," he said, recalling his childhood on the western side of Charleston in a family of five children. Joe's parents divorced when he was five and he went to work at age six out of necessity. Although life was difficult he never asked why his family was poor. Instead, young Joe asked himself, "How can I have a better life?"

Fast-forward to now: Matson Money, a financial coaching firm in Cincinnati, is on track "to cross the threshold of more than $8 billion in assets under management this year," Joe said, referring to the company's growth in 2017. "It took us a long time to make that first $100 million."

Joe is a very successful man—and not just because he is a multimillionaire. His story is about so much more than money. This extraordinary man has a fulfilling life. He is a friend and mentor. I'm sure I learned more from Joe about life and how to succeed than he did from me about golf.

I wanted to learn from Joe, so I asked him the secret to his success. He is living proof that it pays to always give your best effort and ask quality questions.

Joe explained it like this, "If you set your mind to be the best at what you do, so you are proud to put your name on it, you will be successful. I know a janitor who wound up owning the business. He always worked hard and asked quality questions. The janitor didn't ask, 'Why am I just a janitor?' Instead, he asked, 'What do I need to learn to have a better job and career?'

When young Joe was shining the shoes of successful men, he asked questions. He treated these customers as his coaches, and asked them *quality questions*. He would ask questions such as, "How did you get that nice car?" and "What did you do to get started to own your own store?"

He began noticing similarities within each conversation. "The answers almost fell into a pattern," Joe said. "Sometimes a successful man would answer, 'Well, I shined shoes.' Almost always, it started with an education."

The theme of education made a huge impact on Joe. He conveyed to me how his father—the man who dropped out of fifth grade to go to work—loved to read. His father filled a bedroom in the family's home with all kinds of books. "He would read a book a night," Joe recalled.

Through his father's example, advice from successful people and his own interests Joe understood the value of education and learning. He was curious enough to ask the right questions and open minded enough to benefit from the answers. Joe also worked very hard and juggled numerous jobs through his adolescence and young adult years. He eventually found his passion - helping people through financial coaching - and he started Matson Money.

Joe is a living example of using CORE Triumph! to create the life he dreamed about as a child. Through asking questions and reading, he had coaches and mentors. Joe knew his outcome was to be financially secure. And he also had his reasons. Joe didn't want to be poor and struggle to fulfill life's basic needs and he wanted to provide his family a better life. He created an execution plan, adjusted when necessary, and became a multimillionaire. He also takes time to celebrate and enjoy his achievements. Joe's life and his business have an approach to success similar to the four-step plan for CORE Triumph! which involves a coach, an outcome, reasons, and execution.

Your CORE Triumph!™ Plan: Getting Started

What would make you feel fabulous about your golf game? It might be to lower your handicap, to succeed on a shot that was a challenge in the past, to play a round with focus and confidence, to truly enjoy a golf outing, or even to beat your friends. The ideal outcome is different for everyone. Figure out for yourself which result will make you feel energized. This is your time to reach your golf and life goals.

We will develop a CORE Triumph! plan to reach your ideal outcome. This will be a formula you can use to achieve any goal—on the golf course or in life. But first - like Joe - be mindful to ask the right questions in the best way possible.

Why do some people succeed and others fail? The answer is often about the questions they ask themselves. The questions we ask will create a mindset to either remain static or to move forward into triumph.

After a poor golf shot, are you asking, "Why do I even play this game?" or "Why am I still so bad after all these years?" Or are you asking, "How can I improve?" or "How can I refocus to make the next shot better?" Look at your challenge through a positive lens. This will help you believe in yourself and reinforce the fact that you can succeed! Instead of saying, "That was a terrible shot!" say to yourself, "I can do better!"

Next, consider your desired outcome and think about the coaches and mentors you need to surround yourself with in order to succeed. Take a few moments and ask yourself some quality questions: What would be your ideal outcome or result with your golf game? Do you want to lower your handicap? If so, by how many strokes and by when? I've had many students answer this question by saying, "I just don't want to embarrass myself on the golf course. I want to get the ball in the air!" This is a reasonable expectation for new golfers. Maybe you want to win your club championship. If so, then find out some winning scores from the past and whether it is a stroke play or match play format and set those scoring goals. You may be heading to high school and your goal is to make the high-school golf team or to win the county championship. Maybe you want to get a golf scholarship. If so, decide which school you want to attend and determine the scores of current team members. Talk with your coach about your goals.

It is important to be very specific with your goals because the moment you see your outcome clearly, you have taken the first step toward attaining it. This will help prepare you to reach the goals that you set for yourself. It is not my job to define your goals. As your coach, it is my responsibility to guide you and give you the tools to reach your desired outcome.

Let's go through CORE Triumph! for one of your goals. I have included some examples.

Step One: Coach

After you consider a general outcome—like wanting to improve your golf game—write down the coaches and mentors you will need.

Golf Coach: _____

Fitness Coach: _____

Mental-Game Coach: _____

Step Two: Outcome (Goal)

Work with your coach to write down your goals. For example: I want to lower my handicap from 25.2 to 19.8 by six months from today. I want to break 90 as a score within the next three months.

Write the answers to these questions below: What is my ideal outcome? What are the goals I want to achieve in golf?

_____
_____
_____

If your outcome is about shooting a certain score, fantastic. You can do it! But it's important to know that you are not going to do it by actually going out to play with that intention. Focusing on your score during a round of golf will not lead to your best execution. You will learn the tools to play your best golf—one shot at a time—and then the lower scores will happen.

Step Three: Reasons

The next very important step in your CORE Triumph! strategy is to know the reasons you desire this outcome. The *why* is the key ingredient in your motivation and your drive to succeed. Make sure to include every reason and make those reasons as compelling as possible.

Some positive reasons you want to achieve your outcome may include:

- I enjoy golf more when I play well.
- My parents play and I love to spend time with them on the golf course.
- I've always been competitive in other sports and I love that. I want to be better in golf so I can compete again.
- My spouse plays and we love sharing time together on the golf course.
- I love being outside.

Ask yourself the reasons you want the outcome from Step Two and write your answers below.

_____

_____

_____

_____

_____

Step Four: Execution Plan

Now, it's time to create an execution plan and execute it with energy. Sometimes, the challenge in making an action plan is the many other demands on your time. How do you decide where to put your focus and energy every day? Maybe you are not making a conscious effort to be in charge of your 86,400 seconds per day. Maybe you just react to the day's events and go with the flow.

That's why asking the right questions is so important. When you dig deep, understand that you have certain dreams and desires in life and fully grasp the reasons for those goals you will stay focused and committed to your execution plan. When people say they don't have time for something, they are actually saying that "something" is not very important to them. You have heard or spoken sentences such as these before: "I should exercise more, but I don't have the time," or "I really need to practice my short game, but I don't have the time." What you're really saying is "but it's not a priority." Or you're saying something else is just *more* important.

How do we make it mandatory to follow an execution plan? You have taken the first step by writing down the reasons you want to achieve your goals. Take a moment and imagine reaching your goals. What will it feel like to step on the 1st tee with ultimate confidence and excitement? How will you feel walking off the 18th green after shooting your lowest round ever? What will it be like when you are handed the winner's trophy, accept your scholarship, or play a fun round of golf with your family and friends? How will you feel about succeeding in playing a round of golf where you are totally focused and committed on every shot? Close your eyes, imagine your outcome, and feel the emotions.

Let's start writing the plan you will execute. The plan is started below. Add your own ideas to your execution plan to succeed. We will develop even more of the plan throughout this book. I will coach you along the way about what to add to your roadmap to success. Take some time to fill out your execution plan. Fill in the blanks and then continue with more action plans.

Read this book in its entirety and take action where encouraged to do so.

- Practice time: _____
- Play _____ times per week (9 or 18 holes)
- Take lessons from an LPGA or PGA professional
- Start or continue an exercise program _____ days per week

Write down any other execution plans below.

_____

_____

_____

_____

Live Positive!

You have now completed the four steps of CORE Triumph! for your golf game. Let's create a blueprint for another area of your life. This journey is about progress and accomplishment. Progress makes us feel alive! It also feels great to accomplish things in life, and enjoy all the lessons we learn along the way.

Maybe you want to get in better physical shape and lose weight, have an amazing relationship with the love of your life, improve your finances, change your career, focus more on your spirituality, donate more to your favorite charity, or volunteer. Which area of your life would you like to improve? _____

If your health and physical condition is not up to par choose this part of your life to change first. Once you are in better shape you will have more energy, enthusiasm, focus, confidence and determination to tackle another area of life.

Let's start by examining the questions you are asking yourself. Are you asking, "Why can't I lose weight?" or "Why doesn't anyone want to go out with me?" or "Why can't I make more money?" Or are you asking, "What can I do to be healthier?" or "How can I find my perfect mate?" or "What can I do to improve my financial situation?" There is an entire shift in your brain when you are asking questions that will lead to positive answers. Your brain will focus on answering your question. Be sure you are asking the questions that will provide your brain the best substance to produce the desired outcomes. You will find your answers!

Following CORE Triumph! will improve any area of your life that you dream about changing.

Step One: Coach

Above you chose an area of your life you would like to make even better—like getting in great physical shape—write down the coach and mentors you'll need.

_____

_____

_____

Step Two: Outcome (Goal)

Write the answers to these questions: What is my ideal outcome? What are the goals I want to achieve in one area of my life?

_____

_____

_____

_____

Step Three: Reasons

The next very important step in your CORE Triumph! strategy is to know the reasons you want this outcome. The _why_ is the key ingredient in your motivation and your drive to succeed.

Ask yourself the reasons you want the outcome from Step Two and write your answers below.

_____

_____

_____

_____

Step Four: Execution Plan

Now, it's time to create an execution plan and then execute it with energy. Write down your execution plan below.

_____

_____

_____

_____

_____

_____

_____

CORE Triumph!™ Review

Get a *coach*, teacher, or mentor.

Know your *outcome*.

Write down the *reasons* you want to achieve your outcome.

Develop your *execution* plan, and execute it with energy.

Each chapter will have a four-step CORE Triumph! plan for success. It's important that you get comfortable using the process because it will then become part of your daily routine.

Consider following CORE Triumph! in planning discussions with family members and coworkers. If you are a part of a family discussion or a team meeting at the office be prepared by knowing who is the coach or lead person, defining your ideal outcome for the meeting, stating the reasons you want that outcome, and creating a plan to execute for the meeting. You will then have a clear focus for the meeting.

I go through CORE Triumph! every morning. I think about which coaches, mentors, or educators from whom I will learn to keep moving toward my outcome. I take a few moments to visualize my outcome and the reasons I will strive to achieve it. Finally, I write my execution plan for the day and then execute it with energy. I'm ready to start my day.

Imagine taking a few minutes each morning to plan a CORE Triumph! day. Wow! You will accomplish so much each day.

This method will work for you. If you did not write down your coach, outcome, reasons, and plan to execute with energy, go back and take the time to put everything in ink. Take the time to read your CORE Triumph! plan often. Make a vision board with pictures and words (from magazines, posters, personal photos, and so on) to illustrate your CORE Triumph! plan. Display it where you will see it every day. Take time to imagine your outcome as a reality. You get what you focus on in golf and in life, so drown your thoughts in your future achievements.

Chapter 1: Key Elements

Here are the key elements covered in Chapter 1:

- You are on a journey of golf improvement and self-improvement.
- Ask quality questions, in a positive self empowering way
- The four-step plan to Triumph is as follows:
  1. Coach
  2. Outcome
  3. Reasons
  4. Execution
- Educate yourself
- Pay attention to your thoughts and your focus
- Decide which areas in your life you want to make even better
- Use CORE Triumph! daily

Two

The Fundamentals

The minute you get away from fundamentals—
whether it's proper technique, work ethic or mental
preparation—the bottom can fall out of your game,
your schoolwork, your job, whatever you're doing.

—Michael Jordan

In this chapter, we will explore the core fundamentals needed to set yourself up to triumph both on and off the golf course. Below, you will find your CORE Triumph! for this chapter.

Coaches	Outcome	Reasons	Execution
• Debbie O'Connell	• Have a solid foundation	• Have more fun playing	• Read this chapter
• Arnold Palmer	• Hit better golf shots consistently	• Lower scores	• Work through this chapter
• Sally Bowman, CSSD	• Have more energy	• Look like a professional	• Review your golf fundamentals
• David Owen		• Feel confident	• Follow a healthy diet
• Dr. Ara Suppiah		• Live a long healthy life	• Hydrate
		• Spend more quality time with family	• Get enough sleep

The CORE Fundamentals

What are the key fundamentals of golf and life? In golf, as you may already know, the fundamentals are grip, stance, setup, alignment, and equipment. Golf instructors are trained to look at these fundamentals when it's time to analyze an individual's swing. I've given many lessons where I adjusted my student's grip and setup. The student instantly started to hit the ball better. The core components of a sound swing and technique in all shots are basic fundamentals.

I believe in additional fundamentals for success in golf which parallel life choices. For example:

- The amount of sleep you get each night
- Your hydration
- Your nutrition (before and during your round)
- Your clothes
- Your golf fitness—I suggest you find a golf-fitness expert or a professional certified by the Titleist Performance Institute (TPI) for a screening and fitness plan.

Now let's examine all of these core fundamentals for success.

The Technical Fundamentals

Arnold Palmer, considered "The King" of golf, felt so strongly about the fundamentals that he wrote the book, *Play Great Golf: Mastering the Fundamentals.* In an interview with Kelly Tilghman, of the Golf Channel in 2010, Arnold explained that the way he learned the game was simple: Practice the fundamentals of golf and the rest will follow.

When asked what advice he gave to any of his grandchildren who aspired to be professional players, he said, "Learn and practice the fundamentals."[1] We should all heed that advice from one of the greatest golfers to ever play the game.

Whether you are just starting to play golf or you are a seasoned player, it's always important to review the fundamentals. The first technical fundamental I will cover is the grip.

Grip Fundamentals

Your grip is incredibly important. After all, it's how you connect to the golf club. Your grip will influence the position of the clubface at the moment of truth—impact. A proper grip allows you to hinge your wrists, create more power, and support the club at the top of your backswing.

There are a few fundamentals to the golf grip that are true whether you have an interlocking, overlapping, or ten-finger grip.

Interlocking Grip

Overlapping Grip

Ten Finger Grip

1 http://www.golfchannel.com/media/one-one-arnold-palmer/

Your golf club's handle will sit under the pad in the heel of your glove or lead hand (left for the right-handed golfer and right for the left-handed golfer), and your fingers will hold it. As you wrap your hand to hold the handle, be sure you see two or three knuckles on that lead hand as you look down at your grip. Place your trail hand on the handle with your palm facing the target. Allow the thumb of your lead hand to nestle in the palm and along the lifeline of your trail hand.

When you look down at your grip, you will see the two or three knuckles—but not the thumb—of your lead hand.

Take a moment to check your grip and grip pressure. Remember, this is your only contact with the club. It's not uncommon for a professional to use the analogy of feeling as if you are holding a bird in your hands. Please don't kill the bird! Another way to understand grip pressure is to imagine you are holding a tube of toothpaste upside down with the cap off. Your grip should be light enough that you won't squeeze out the contents. Many of my students feel as if the golf club will fly out of their hands if they hold it softly, so I have a solution which I call "The Secret:" Hold on a little tighter with the pinky and ring finger of your lead hand and you will feel secure that you won't lose the club.

I have a quick story about grip pressure. I was encouraging one of my students to loosen her grip pressure and she commented that she felt as if the club were going to fly out of her hands. I reassured her she would not let the club fly out of her hands. At the time, I didn't know about the secret of holding a little tighter with the pinky and ring finger. A couple days later, she walked into the pro shop and I immediately asked her how she played. She said, "Well, I loosened my grip and played better, but my 7-iron is in the woods on the left side of the 5th fairway!" Oops! Be sure to implement "The Secret."

Setup Fundamentals

Let's take some time to check your setup fundamentals. A proper setup will allow you to make your most powerful golf swing. Keep your back straight and bend forward from the hips. Think of the forward bend as a *tush push* because of where your backside goes as you bend forward; however, be careful not to round your upper back or arch your lower back. This sounds easy, but many of my students struggle with this forward bend. Simply stand up straight and bend forward from the hips. Your backswing rotation will be impeded if you arch your lower back or round your upper back, which usually results in many swing flaws.

A proper posture and setup will be more effective when your back is in a neutral position, as noted in these photos.

| Rounded Back | Arched Back | Neutral Back |

Think of the forward tilt like this: You have just arrived home from grocery shopping and you want to carry all of the bags into the house in one trip. Your arms are full, but you have to close the car door. What do you do? Obviously, you stand with your back to the car door and then quickly bend and *bam*, your backside hits the door and it slams shut. This is the tush push.

After the tush push, allow your arms to hang from your shoulders. This is where you will grip the club. Avoid reaching out from your body, which will cause tension in your arms and shoulders. I call this part of the setup *tilt and hang*.

Now, take some time to review your setup in a mirror with a golf club. Look into the mirror face on, tilt forward, and let your arms hang. Go ahead and grip the club, setting your hands in front of the inner thigh of your lead leg. Check your balance. You should feel sturdy enough that someone couldn't knock you over with a slight push. Now, look in the mirror from the side to ensure that your back is neutral. From this position, tilt your pelvis back and forth while keeping your upper back still. This move will test the muscles you will use during your golf swing. If you cannot make this movement, I suggest finding a fitness professional with golf-fitness training to help you. If you can make the move but feel shaking, repeat the pelvis tilt three times a week for ten repetitions to strengthen those muscles. This exercise will help you rotate more efficiently around your spine when it is in the tilted position.

BALL-POSITION FUNDAMENTALS

Let's review ball position relative to your stance at setup. There are general guidelines about ball position, but there are factors that make it unique to each golfer. Contributing factors include flexibility, size, strength, shape of swing, speed of swing, and desired outcome. If your desired outcome is to lower your handicap, I suggest spending time with an LPGA or PGA professional who is equipped with today's technology. Your professional will be able to help you find the best ball positions for the various clubs that you will swing. You may need to experiment a little, but here is a guideline for the ball position relative to the various clubs you will hit:

- **Driver:** This club has the most forward ball position (toward your lead foot) of all clubs because it is the longest club, with the intent to hit the ball on the upswing. Hitting the ball on the upswing launches the ball higher with less spin and creates more distance. I'm sure the two words "more distance" excite you as much as they excite me. Play the ball somewhere between your lead armpit (faster club speeds) and just outside your lead shoulder (slower club speeds).

- **Fairway Woods and Hybrids:** You want to strike the ball at or very near the bottom of the arc of your swing, not on the upswing or downswing. The most effective ball position is the width of two golf balls forward (toward the target) of the center of your stance.

- **Irons:** You want to strike the ball in your downswing when hitting with an iron. Typically, the ball is played in the center of your stance for short irons to middle irons, and the width of one golf ball forward of center for the 6-iron and higher. The great news is that you can stop trying to force yourself to hit down on the ball with your irons. Just make a golf swing with proper ball position, and your iron will strike the ball during the downward path. Whew! That's one less thing to think about.

I know, I know—going over grip, setup, and ball position for you more experienced golfers seems boring. But if you haven't checked these fundamentals recently, please take the time—it's worth it. Remember what Arnold Palmer said about fundamentals, "Fundamentals are what the best players in the world work on." They are the foundation—yes, the CORE—of a great golf swing. Now is the time to reach your goals. So let's make sure you get off to a fantastic start.

The Physical Fundamentals for Golf and Life

We all need sleep, water, food, and shelter to survive. But if we want to thrive, we need to understand how much sleep and water we need, and the best types of food for peak performance. For our purposes, shelter includes clothing, headgear, and sunscreen.

Sleep: The Winner's Secret

It's time to meet your sleep coaches: David Owen, a contributing editor for *Golf Digest*, and Dr. Ara Suppiah, of the Golf Channel.

In April 2012, David published, "My Tech: Sleep Better, Play Better." In the column, he points out that research shows sleep—or the lack of it—affects "such rest-dependent factors as focus, temper control and 'executive function,' which are crucial to playing golf." He recommends cell phone apps to help monitor your sleep habits, so you will know exactly how much sleep you are getting each night.[2]

I love my Fitbit Charge HR for many reasons, but I find it very interesting to monitor my sleep patterns. It shows me the number of hours I slept, times

2 http://video.golfdigest.com/watch/david-owen-stuff-i-like-august-2012

I was restless, and times I was awake. Perhaps you can study yourself and determine the number of hours of sleep you need to be at your best. If you have severe insomnia or sleep apnea, you may need to undergo an overnight study performed in a hospital or a sleep center.

According to WebMD, sleep apnea is a disorder that causes interruptions in nighttime breathing, serious sleep problems, and loud snoring. While it often affects middle-aged men, women can also be affected. I know a few people who have sleep apnea. The difference in their energy and stamina once it was diagnosed and treated was tremendous. If you have any indication you may have sleep apnea, please contact your doctor.[3]

How much sleep do you need to play your best golf? Your ideal sleep time will be unique—just like you. Most physicians recommend seven or eight hours of sleep a night. As David wrote in his *Golf Digest* column, "Of course, no two golfers are alike. Tiger Woods is said to sleep just four or five hours a night. Michelle Wie tries for ten or twelve." I fit right in the middle, needing seven to eight hours to feel completely rested and ready to start my day.

The experts at the Golf Channel agree sleep is crucial to playing your best golf. "Sleep is 'free medicine,'" said Dr. Suppiah, a medical contributor to the *Morning Drive*, the Golf Channel's daily news-and-lifestyle program; and to *Golf Central*, the network's evening news show. He is a lifelong athlete and a personal physician for several top PGA and LPGA Tour professionals, including Justin Rose, Vijay Singh, Anna Nordqvist, and Julieta Granada. You can visit Dr. Suppiah's web page on the Golf Channel's website for more information.[4]

HYDRATION

Water is the drink of life. Our bodies are about 60 to 70 percent water. Without water, the kidneys and other major organs will fail. Simply put, we can't survive without water. Beyond survival, water also plays a crucial role in

---

3 http://www.m.webmd.com/sleep-disorders/sleep-apnea

4 http://www.golfchannel.com/about/bio/dr-ara-suppiah/

hydration—one of the fundamentals we need to focus on for health and performance on and off the golf course.

Let's meet our hydration coach, Sally Bowman. She is a registered and licensed dietitian who is also a certified specialist in sports dietetics (CSSD) with Central Texas Nutrition Consultants, in Austin, Texas.[5] For ten years, she was a sports dietitian for the University of Texas Athletics Department. Her published work includes guidance on nutrition and health for golfers.[6]

"Drinking enough water and other fluids will help you avoid injuries during a round of golf," Sally said. "Hydrated muscles can handle more stress without injury. Imagine a raw steak and what happens when you pull off a piece…imagine what happens with beef jerky." None of us want to think about our muscles in beef-jerky mode. Sally said muscles are 80 percent water, which is just one reason why it's important to keep drinking water and other fluids before, during, and after a round of golf or any other workout. It's worth repeating: Staying hydrated will help protect you from injury.

On the flip side, dehydration can be ugly—for your golf score and your health. One day, I was giving a lesson on a very hot summer day to a lady who was in her early seventies. She had quite a medical history, so I was watching her closely. About ten minutes into the lesson, I noticed she was moving slowly and couldn't focus very well. I asked whether she was feeling OK. She said she was fine. I asked her how much water she drank that morning. She shared that she had only had a few swallows while taking her medicine. After handing her a cup of water, I suggested we go inside to review her lesson plan. She agreed and said she wanted to shop for a new putter anyway. I immediately got a chair for her when we arrived in the air-conditioned golf shop. She sat down and passed out. When the EMT asked her about her medical history, she said, "I look much better in person than I do on paper!" I laughed and knew she was feeling better. As they rolled her out on the stretcher, she put her arm in the air and said, "Hey, Debbie, same time next week for a lesson?" I chuckled and said I would call her.

---

5 http://www.austin-nutritiontherapy.net/
6 http://www.golfaustin.org/my-golf/nutrition-and-health-for-golfers/sports-nutrition-for-golfers/

Sally said besides raising the risk of injury, dehydration can lead to a host of unwanted consequences. Dehydration can lower endurance, lessen strength and power, decrease your body's ability to cool itself, reduce blood flow to your working muscles, lower concentration, and slow recovery from and increase risk of heat cramping and other heat-related illnesses. Swollen feet and headache are among the more minor—but still significant—problems dehydration can cause.

This is definitely not good for your golf game or daily life. Drink up, people!

Now that we know what can go wrong without good hydration, let's look at how to get it right. The best approach to staying hydrated is the one that's tailored for your body and activity level, according to Sally.

Sally explains that weather—temperature and humidity, specifically—affects the amount of water and other liquids you will need to stay hydrated while out on the links. When I play golf on a hot, humid day, I make a magic formula of water, lemon, and Himalayan pink salt. According to my nutritionist, Himalayan pink salt is naturally filled with electrolytes and much better for you than Gatorade, which has a lot of sugar.

"In cold weather, you still need water," Sally notes. "Thirst is not a good indicator of hydration. Thirst may be telling you something. But it's past the point where you need to be drinking. You need another indication of your level of hydration."

Since two of my favorite beers are Guinness® and Michelob ULTRA, I really like Sally's beer color-wheel test for urine. "To monitor your hydration level, you must notice the color of your urine," Sally said. "Golf and beer go together. I like to compare the urine colors to types of beer. If you're hydrated, your urine stays lightly colored, like Michelob ULTRA. As you move toward less hydration, the color might be something like a pilsner or an IPA. As you become more under hydrated, you move toward an amber. If you're at a Guinness® level, you're probably going to land in the hospital!"

To find out whether you are hydrated, you should urinate every two to three hours and pay attention to the color of your urine.

NUTRITION: EAT LIKE A WINNER

Nutrition is the energy you need to function. We can compare it to putting gasoline in your car. I like to put premium fuel into my body. I've learned so much from many great nutritionists and life experiences.

Years ago, I was playing a practice round before a national tournament and I was playing great. I experienced fourteen well-played holes. All of a sudden, my timing was off and I struggled during the final four holes. One of my playing partners asked me whether I had eaten anything during my round of golf that day and I answered no. She said, "Well, that explains what happened on the last four holes. You were playing great up until then!" Wow, did I learn a big lesson.

The next day, during the first round of the tournament, I arrived at the golf course with nuts, an apple, and a banana. The tournament host also provided peanut butter and jelly sandwiches at three different holes during the event. I ate at least a quarter of a sandwich every time I passed a sandwich station and I ate my snacks in between. When I started eating my third sandwich, my caddie, who was one of my students, looked at me in disbelief and asked, "Are you still hungry?"

I laughed and said, "No, I just don't want to run out of fuel!"

Food and water give you energy. In order to play your best golf, you want to fill your body with proper nutrition and plenty of water. Now, I'm not a nutritionist, but I've read many books and studies on the subject and learned a great deal from nutrition experts. Studies prove that a healthy diet improves energy, focus, and overall health.

In general, eat mostly live foods—vegetables and fruit. Ingest your proteins from lean meats - like fish, chicken and turkey - nuts, nut butters (I love almond butter), and seeds; get your carbohydrates from whole grains, beans, sweet potatoes, lentils, peas, brown rice, and quinoa; and ingest your healthy fats from avocado, olive oil, nuts (such as walnuts, almonds, hazelnuts, and pecans), and fish.

Foods to avoid in your healthy diet include white flour, refined sugars, white rice, and pasta, as well as dairy products. According to WebMD, white foods are considered to be the "bad carbs." The site goes on to explain, "A study in 2004 showed that people who ate too many refined carbs were at increased risk for obesity and type 2 diabetes."[7] On the other hand, eating whole grains slows absorption so there is no spike in insulin. Whole grains also help to meet your fiber needs.

Having a hot dog, a bag of chips, and a beer or a soda at the turn, which is after the completion of the first nine holes where a snack bar or the clubhouse is often located, may be what you look forward to during a round of golf, but they are not the best choices for peak performance. Most golf courses are attempting to provide healthier choices for golfers, but don't count on it. Make your own plan for a smart diet that will give you energy and focus during your round of golf. Pack some nuts (such as walnuts, almonds, and pecans), some fruit (such as apples, bananas, pears, and oranges), and some raw vegetables (such as carrots, celery, and cucumbers). Instead of that hot dog, bring a "nut butter" and jelly sandwich on 100 percent whole grain bread. Or, even better, use Ezekiel bread. Be sure to eat something every three to four holes for optimum energy and focus during your entire round.

SODIUM

A couple of years ago, I noticed that I would get dizzy if I stood up quickly. I would pause for a moment as I saw a spattering of black. In a few seconds, it would go away, and I would feel fine. When I mentioned this to my doctor, she asked whether I consumed much salt. I told her that I didn't because I thought salt wasn't good for you. She informed me that only those with high blood pressure should be cautious of their salt intake. My blood pressure is low, so I need some salt in my diet.

According to Sally, you must replenish the sodium that your body eliminates during sweat loss. Salt is also known as sodium chloride. Sodium helps regulate water in the body. It is one of the electrolytes. Electrolytes are salts and minerals that conduct the body's electrical signals, firing up your muscles and running your brain. Sodium and other electrolytes also play a vital role in the body's fluid balance, energy level, and biochemistry. I use Himalayan pink salt for the electrolytes it provides.

---

7 http://www.m.webmd.com/diet/features/truth-about-white-foods

The nuun* brand (pronounced "noon") of electrolyte tablets is popular now, Sally says, adding, "I've had runners say they prefer these tablets to Gatorade."

Electrolytes include seven major elements: sodium, chloride, potassium, magnesium, calcium, phosphate, and bicarbonate. Let's take a look at one of the most important electrolytes, potassium. Why is potassium important? "Potassium is involved in just about every physiological reaction in moving fluid in and out of the cells, including every heartbeat," according to WebMD.[8]

"A fresh piece of fruit, such as a banana, orange, or grape, is another healthy way to keep your carbohydrate and electrolyte levels up during exercise," Sally says.

SHELTER

Another golf fundamental is your clothing on the golf course. You might be wondering why I mention clothing as part of the fundamentals. I like the expression, "If you look good, you play good!" You will get a boost of confidence by wearing clothing that fits you well, is perfect for the weather conditions, and makes you feel confident.

Years ago, I was playing in the LPGA Teaching and Club Professional (T&CP) National Championship. In preparation, I bought a few new golf outfits. After all, I wanted to look good. I was thrilled with the colors and how they fit. On the morning of the first round, I was warming up on the driving range and noticed that my shirt collar didn't sit right. It kept getting in my way during my setup and swing. I had a bit of a challenge. I asked the staff member at the range whether he had a pair of scissors handy and, luckily, he did—in his Swiss Army knife. I asked him if he would mind cutting the part of my shirt that was interfering with my swing and my focus. He obliged. When I shared this story with my good friend Teresa after my round, she laughed and said something similar had happened to her during a tournament. When she got into her setup for her first tee shot, she realized she couldn't get her legs wide enough in her stance for the driver without having her brand new skirt

---

8 http://www.webmd.com/heart-disease/potassium-and-your-heart#1

slide up to the tops of her thighs. She had to narrow her stance for the rest of the day. We both learned that we should take a new outfit for a "test-drive" before playing in an important golf tournament.

The final word about clothing is simple: Always be prepared. In the cooler months, keep winter gloves, a jacket, a warm hat, and hand warmers in your golf bag. You may also want to put a rain suit in your bag, as well as an umbrella, extra golf gloves, and towels. You may sense your golf bag getting heavier with every item I'm suggesting. It's worth the extra weight. Preparation is a key to success. Picture a scenario where you are playing a great round. It begins to rain and you are not prepared. As a result, your round suffers. It wasn't the conditions, but instead the *lack of preparation* for those conditions that prevented you from shooting a low score.

SUNSCREEN: PROTECT YOUR SKIN LIKE A WINNER

My dermatologist stressed to me that the risk of skin cancer could be reduced by diligently and consistently protecting myself from ultraviolet sun rays. She also asked me to make an appointment every six months as she explained early detection is a key to staying cancer-free.

Golfers are particularly vulnerable to sun damage to their skin. Find a sunscreen that works for you and use it religiously on every exposed inch of skin, from your hairline down. You don't want to undergo surgery to remove precancerous or malignant spots from your face, ears, neck, hands, or elsewhere.

The Skin Cancer Foundation recommends that you apply one ounce of sunscreen to your body—about the size of a golf ball—and reapply every two hours after swimming or excessive sweating. Use a sunscreen with SPF (sun protection factor) 15 or higher.[9]

Skin cancer is one of the most preventable types of cancer. It is also among the easiest types of cancer to treat—if it's detected and treated early. Remember to protect your lips as well as your skin; be sure your lip balm includes sunscreen.

---

9 http://www.skincancer.org/prevention/sun-protection/prevention-guidelines/preventing-skin-cancer

There are fundamental aspects in everyday life. To be your best each day—whether you're going to work or spending time with family—it's important to take care of yourself. You will get the most out of life if you have enough sleep, energy, focus, hydration, sodium, nutrition, shelter, and sunscreen.

Chapter 2: Key Elements

Here are the key elements covered in Chapter 2:

Set yourself up for success in golf and in life by checking your fundamentals. Take a moment to review each of the items listed below and fill in the blank or check off the item when you are confident your fundamental is correct:

_____ Grip

_____ Setup

_____ Ball position

_____ Prepared for inclement weather

_____ Bring healthy snacks to the golf course

_____ Wear sunscreen

_____ Reapply sunscreen

_____ Hours of sleep needed for optimal performance

_____ Number of ounces of water per day for optimal performance

_____ Compare urine color to beer color wheel

_____ Avoid white bread, white rice and pasta

_____ Set myself up for success with core fundamentals every day

Three

PREPARE

One important key to success is self-confidence. An important key to self-confidence is preparation.

—ARTHUR ASHE

By reading and following the actions in this chapter, you will learn and understand how to prepare to hit a golf ball. Together, you and I will examine how to prepare yourself to start each day and give you strategies to make each day count.

Coaches	Outcome	Reasons	Execution
• Debbie O'Connell	• Have an effective pre-shot routine	• Be totally prepared to execute each shot on the golf course	• Read this chapter
• Pia Nilsson	• Create clarity to gain confidence in all shots	• Feel great about the round, knowing you gave each shot your best	• Practice pre-shot routines for golf and life
• Lynn Marriott	• Start each day with energy	• Be more consistent	• Pay attention to mental-focus and physical-tension levels
		• Play better golf	• Use CORE Triumph! every morning, and be ready to start the day
		• Make the most of every day and be truly thankful	
		• Handle any stressful situation with confidence	

Preparation is a key to success. Preparing for each and every shot on the golf course is a key to lower scores. How you prepare is crucial to the process of playing even better golf.

Pia Nilsson and Lynn Marriott are fellow LPGA professionals and friends of mine. They are well-known instructors who cofounded VISION54. According to vision54.com, "VISION54 is many things. It's a number, a philosophy, an attitude, a process, and a discipline. It represents a future full of possibilities and unlimited human potential." It's Pia and Lynn's business, and they are teaching both amateur and professional golfers to be their best. A small nugget of their teaching includes a preparation process that has proven to be successful. Pia coached Annika Sorenstam, the world's best female golfer during her career on the LPGA Tour, and Annika credits much of her success to VISION54 (Nilsson and Marriott 2005).

VISION54 teaches a pre-shot routine that includes standing in an area behind the golf ball called the *Think Box*, where you analyze the situation, plan the shot you want to hit, visualize that shot, choose the club, and pick your target. You take your practice swing in this area as well. As you watch golf on television, you will notice that professional golfers stand behind the golf ball to make their decisions and choose a target, maybe talk with their caddie, and visualize the exact shot they plan to execute.

Once all of the thinking is complete and you are totally committed to the shot, you will step over the imaginary *Decision Line* into the *Play Box*. Here is where you get into your setup, take one more look at the target (I like to add that you should take a deep breath and release any tension in your body at this point), and then swing. You don't want to spend too much time in the *Play Box*. This is where you take action—without thinking. Sometimes it's hard not to think, so I will say a word such as "yes" or "target" just before I swing as I look at and engage with the target one last time.

I recall one round of golf I was playing with the great Nancy Lopez, a member of both the LPGA Tour and World Golf Halls of Fame. Nancy and I were partners against two other professionals. We were playing a better-ball format, which means we each played our own ball, and we each had a score. The lowest score between Nancy and me was our team score. We were on a long par-5 at PGA National and Nancy hit her ball into a fairway bunker. She continued to struggle on the hole—a rare occurrence, as she had carried me most of the day. I hit two good shots, but a strong wind was blowing directly into us, which left me a shot playing almost 200 yards into the green, where I wanted to hit the ball. Recently, I had been struggling with my fairway wood, but with that wind, I needed it to reach the green in regulation (three shots on a par-5). Our opponents were in good shape on the hole, but Nancy needed me to come through for our team. I was feeling the pressure and my heart was beating quickly; I couldn't let Nancy down. I started my pre-shot routine and when I stepped over the *Decision Line* into the *Play Box*, I kept repeating the word "target" in my head. I didn't want to allow any doubt or negative thoughts to enter my mind. I knew that engaging with the target would help me swing better. With my heart beating and my mind engaged with the target, I made my swing and then watched my ball fly into the air and land on the green. I was so excited and relieved. I two-putted for par and we halved the hole (tied with the other team).

If you do not have a pre-shot routine, you will want to develop one. Spend time practicing that routine at the practice range so you don't have to think about it on the golf course. To be the most effective, your pre-shot routine will include the *Think Box*, *Decision Line*, and *Play Box* areas.

You always want to stand behind the golf ball, in line with your target, and then find something on the ground (a divot, stick, leaf) that is about two feet in front of the ball and in line with your target. Then, when you approach the ball to get into your setup, aim the face of your club at the spot you picked on the ground. It's much easier to aim properly at something that is two feet in front of you than something 200 yards away.

After your club is lined up, picture an imaginary line from your target back to your ball—that's the target line—and set your feet parallel to the imaginary line. You can see how important finding a spot on your target line is in helping you align yourself correctly as you get into your setup position.

Pia and Lynn share a story in their book *Every Shot Must Have a Purpose* about Annika Sorenstam during the 2004 U.S. Women's Open. She came to a short par-4, chose her club, and teed up her golf ball. When she realized that there was still a group on the fairway and she couldn't tee off yet, she picked up her ball and tee, walked back to her bag, put her club back in the bag, and put the head cover back on the club. This allowed Annika to get back to the *Think Box* and mentally reload.

I was in a situation similar to Annika's in a golf tournament many years ago. It was not the U.S. Women's Open, but it was a professional tournament.

I arrived at the tee, pulled out my driver, placed the ball on the tee, and then noticed there was a group on the fairway. Instead of going back to my bag and putting my club away as Annika did, I stayed on the tee box, waiting for the group to move on. As I waited, I took a few extra swings and tried to fight the negative thoughts that wanted to enter my mind. When the fairway was clear, I did my practice swing, picked my target, and set up to the ball. Then I proceeded to hit the golf ball out of bounds. Annika hit her shot to her target. It was a wonderful learning experience for me!

Let's take a moment to talk about targets. First, you want to have a target for every shot. I will often ask a player, "What is your target?" and the response will be something like "down there" or "the middle of the fairway" or "the green." In choosing your target, it's best to choose a very specific target, such as the left edge of the bunker, the tree behind the green, the flag, or a spot on the green to land a chip shot. The more specific you are in defining your target, the more clarity there will be in the shot you plan to execute.

Also, pick a target that gives you room to be successful. By "successful," I mean that even if your ball does not go exactly where you've planned, there is still room to the left and right of the target for your ball to land in a good position. Jack Nicklaus once said, "I hit five or six perfect shots per round. The rest are just good misses." That's coming from one of the best players—if not *the* best player—to ever step on the links.[10]

You may already have a pre-shot routine and that is fantastic. Be sure to incorporate the *Think Box, Decision Line,* and *Play Box* in addition to choosing a target and a spot for alignment from behind the ball. Based on your preference, you can decide whether to take a practice swing. Most golfers take one. I recommend it, but it's not mandatory. If you do take a practice swing, be sure to make it a real swing. It is supposed to be practice for the shot you are about to hit. Often, I see a player make a half swing or a slow-motion swing for practice, but that's not as effective as taking a real swing.

---

10 http://www.golfswingsecretsrevealed.com/blog/2009/10/04/the-most-important-48-shots-in -golf/

Again, to be more consistent with successful golf shots, you want to improve both your physical swing and your mental strategies. There is more information about the physical swing later in this book. First, let's focus on having a pre-shot routine with a *Think Box*, a *Decision Line*, and a *Play Box* that will get you mentally prepared to make a great swing.

Live Positive!

How do you prepare for each day of your life? Do you have a pre-day routine that gets you mentally prepared? Do you have morning rituals? I bet you do, but are they getting you what you want in life?

Maybe your ritual is to hit the snooze button over and over again until you realize you only have ten minutes to get ready. This ritual will barely give you enough time to brush your teeth. There's no time to plan the day (if you planned it the night before, that's awesome), eat a healthy breakfast, or take a breath. You may be causing yourself unnecessary stress because of the last two pushes of the snooze button.

Let's examine the morning rituals of a few of the most successful people in the world. *Business Insider* says that Jack Dorsey, the CEO of Twitter and Square, wakes up at five o'clock in the morning, meditates for thirty minutes, does three seven-minute workouts, and then checks in with his companies.[11]

Sir Richard Branson, whose net worth is over $5 billion, wakes up at five o'clock in the morning, exercises (he swims, kite surfs, or plays tennis), spends time with his family, and then gets to work. "Over my 50 years in business I have learned that if I rise early I can achieve so much more in a day, and therefore in life," he says.[12]

Arianna Huffington, the co-founder and former editor-in-chief of *The Huffington Post*—now owned by AOL—wakes up early, takes time to breathe deeply, does thirty minutes of meditation, and sets her intentions for the day.

---

11 http://www.businessinsider.com/jack-dorsey-wakes-up-at-5-in-the-morning-to-mediate-2015-12

12 http://www.businessinsider.com/what-everyone-can-learn-from-richard-bransons-morning-routine-2015-10

What I've learned in life is if you desire another person's success, then you should follow his or her lead. As I read about the morning rituals of successful entrepreneurs, I noticed a pattern of rising early, meditating, and exercising.

The world is filled with challenges, mishaps, and negative people and circumstances. It's up to you to arm yourself with positive energy, confidence, and motivation to truly make the most of each and every day.

I also researched the morning rituals of happy people. According to Kickvick, there are seven morning habits of healthy and happy people:[13]

1. They begin anew.
2. They wake with a sense of gratitude.
3. They read something positive.
4. They use self-inquiry to affirm a purposeful start to the day. For example, Steve Jobs used to start by looking in the mirror and asking, "If today were the last day of my life, would I want to do what I am about to do today?"[14]
5. They give themselves time to eat a wholesome breakfast.
6. They follow a morning routine. In my research, I found that most routines included exercise.
7. They move on gracefully to what's most important.

You are in charge of your daily habits and rituals. A great morning ritual can get you in a peak state of mind as well as a positive emotional state. Start your day off in the best way possible to prepare yourself to focus on your outcome and execution plan so you can hit your targets in life. Just as in golf, get into a good state, and choose your target for the day.

Every morning, I take a few minutes and think about the things that I am thankful for in my life. I start with my family and friends—those I love and who love me back. I'll think about things like being able to see, hear, talk and walk. Then, I think of a few simple items that make life amazing. One

---

13 http://www.kickvick.com/morning-habits/

14 http://projectlifemastery.com/morning-rituals-of-tony-robbins-oprah-steve-jobs-lady-gaga/

morning, the thought of a chair came to mind, and I thought, "Wow, I'm so thankful we have chairs to sit on." My mind quickly went to all kinds of chairs and the places I use them such as the movie theater, the dinner table, sports stadiums, airplanes and so many more. My mind then started going back to when I was younger, sitting in school, in a car seat, in a stroller, and then I remembered the greatest seat ever: Before I could walk, I had a chair with wheels so I could walk and run. I started to laugh and thought, "Thank you!"

After my moments of gratitude, I think about the day ahead. I go through my CORE Triumph! strategy and ask myself the following questions:

- Who are my Coaches?
- What is my Outcome for today?
- What are my Reasons for the Outcome?

Do you remember what Joe Matson taught us in the first chapter about asking quality questions? These questions are a key to accomplishing all of your goals. And then I review my Execution plan and get really excited to execute with energy.

Before I get out of bed, I feel so happy and filled with gratitude, and I'm totally excited to get up and live my life to the fullest. After that, I stand up tall and confident like a superhero and yell to my pets, "Who's ready to start the day?"

Next in my daily ritual is to take my dog, Mickey, for a walk, jog, and run. Being fit, healthy, and full of energy is my standard, so starting my day with activity is a must.

Mickey and me on our walk

What is your standard for each day of your life? Are you willing to just get up and go with the flow? Will you let the challenges of the day get you down? Or will you take charge of your life, thoughts, feelings, and emotions, and make each day a progression toward your ultimate life? Will you stay focused on your desired outcome, no matter what happens in the day?

The best way to reach higher standards is to have a pre-day routine that gets you into a state ready for peak performance.

Write down your pre-day routine to Triumph each morning.

1. _____
2. _____
3. _____
4. _____

Chapter 3: Key Elements

Here are the key elements covered in Chapter 3:

- Have a pre-shot routine that includes the *Think Box*, the *Decision Line*, and the *Play Box*.
- Take charge of your day each and every morning with your pre-day routine. It should include:
  - Gratitude
  - CORE Triumph!
  - Total excitement to start the day
  - Exercise
  - A healthy breakfast

Four

Backswing Consistency

If there is one thing I have learned during my
years as a professional, it is that the only thing
constant about golf is its inconsistency.

—Jack Nicklaus

In this chapter, you will gain insights and drills to help you create techniques
that make it easier to be more consistent. You will learn from blind golfer
Jake Olson that this is not a game of hand-eye coordination, but one of creating repeatable movements.

We will also examine your habits—what you do consistently in your life.
I'll coach you on breaking bad habits and on creating new empowering habits
that will lead you to Triumph.

Coaches
- Debbie O'Connell
- Jake Olson
- Charles Duhigg
- Tony Robbins

Outcome
- Develop more consistent, well-played shots
- Improve techniques in putting and chipping
- Consistently experience great days

Reasons
- Lower golf scores
- Execute well consistently
- Beat your friends
- Win tournaments
- Enjoy life even more

Execution
- Read this chapter
- Work through this chapter
- Practice putting, chipping, and full-swing techniques in the mirror
- Pay attention to whether thoughts are positive or negative
- Have an attitude of gratitude

Jack Nicklaus is absolutely correct about the inconsistency of the game of golf. The game is unpredictable. Despite this, there are components of the game that can narrow the mistakes you make during a round of golf. Let's make your misses better by improving your swing.

The golf swing is more about rhythm, tempo, and timing than it is about having a stick and smacking a ball. The approach of smacking the ball makes it challenging to be consistent. A more effective strategy is to develop a consistent movement pattern rather than relying on hand-eye coordination. Blind people play golf, which proves that you don't have to see the ball to make contact. Jake Olson is a blind golfer who dreams of playing on the PGA Tour.

Let me tell you about Jake. He was born with a rare form of eye cancer called retinoblastoma. Before he was a year old, he had lost his left eye to cancer. He fought the disease for twelve years, going through chemotherapy each time it returned. But his doctors ultimately had to take out his right eye. Jake became completely blind at twelve years old.

Before he lost his sight, he played golf and football. After he went blind, Jake wanted to play football so badly that he asked himself what position he could play that wouldn't require him to see. Remember, in Chapter 1, when we talked about asking quality questions? Jake found the answer—he could be a long snapper. When he first started, he was not very good at all. The coach put him on the team but thought there was no way Jake could play. Jake then asked the coach what he could do to improve. Jake didn't lament about what he could no longer do. He listened to his coach and worked so hard he became a starter.

"Brokenness doesn't exist in the body. It exists in the mind, body, and spirit. Mine remains whole!" Jake said.[15]

As for golf, his goal is to be the first blind golfer on the PGA Tour. He says, "Since I've become blind, I see better than ever what my true potential can be." Jake is the author of the book *Open Your Eyes: 10 Uncommon Lessons to Discover a Happier Life.*[16] We can learn so much from this courageous young man.

Jake is able to play golf because the golf ball is not moving, so it doesn't require hand-eye coordination. Playing well does require him to trust his golf swing and create a repeatable move. As I watched his swing, I noticed how he used his big muscles, making it easy to be consistent. He used his upper back and shoulders in his backswing, and he used his legs, glutes, and core at the top of his swing all the way to the finish. Jake has a consistent swing.

When I ask my students what their goals are, the answer I get most often is that they desire to be more consistent. Truly, you are more consistent than you realize. The movement you make in your swing is usually the same except for something very minor.

---

15 http://www.openyoureyes.org/jake-olson
16 Olsen, Jake and McKay Christensen, *Open Your Eyes: 10 Uncommon Lessons to Discover a Happier Life* (Tennessee: Nelson Books, 2013).

The key to consistency is to use your big muscles. You'll notice when you watch LPGA or PGA Tour professionals putt, the club swings back and through because of the movement of the upper back and shoulders. Their arms, hands, and club swing like a pendulum back and through. The larger muscles can consistently swing the club back and through. If your wrists are the catalyst of the movement, it's more difficult to hit the shot consistently well. Think of the amount of movement in all different directions that the wrists can cause. Now imagine a proper setup with your eyes over your ball, using your shoulders to swing your putter. As long as you keep your head still, the club will swing consistently.

In your full swing, a complete shoulder turn is key. You will make your best takeaway by starting to move the golf club with your upper back and lead shoulder. This will get you started with a one-piece takeaway, which is when your shoulders, arms, hands, and golf club all start moving away from the target at the same time and at the same tempo.

Let me just mention that there are many successful golfers who make their first move in their backswing with their hands and wrists. Kenny Perry is a great example. He has grooved a swing where he hinges his wrists first and then turns his shoulders and hips. Perry has fourteen wins on the PGA Tour and eight more on the PGA Tour Champions, so there is no arguing with success. As a professional golfer, Perry spends a tremendous amount of time creating a very consistent, repeatable golf swing.

I have found that many of my students who make their first move with their wrists do not make a full shoulder turn and they are inconsistent in their timing. By getting your shoulders moving immediately, you will continue to move them and set yourself up for a full shoulder turn and a powerful swing.

Here's a drill you can try: Place two golf balls on the ground on the target line (the imaginary line from your target to your golf ball), about six inches apart. Address the ball that is closest to the target (*photo 1*). Begin your takeaway by pushing with your lead shoulder and arm, allowing the clubhead to stay low to the ground and hit the other ball backward as you make your shoulder turn (*photo 2*). Continue your swing and hit the front ball. The goal of this drill is to keep you from lifting the golf club up with your hands and arms for your backswing. If you lift the golf club, you may leave out the shoulder turn and lose a lot of power.

Photo 1   Photo 2

Chip to Improve Consistency

There's a shot in golf that, when you practice it correctly, improves every part of your game. You are probably thinking, "Seriously, Debbie, one shot that helps everything?" Yes! Practicing the chip shot—or the bump and run or the chip and run, whatever you may call it—will not only improve your chip shot, but will also improve your putting, your pitch shot, your full swing, your sand shot, your punch shot—everything. You are probably curious. How can one shot help everything else in the game?

In chipping, we are going to focus on using your big muscles in your upper back and shoulders. It is easier to feel the technique in a shorter swing because there are fewer moving parts and you are not trying to hit the ball far. Using your big muscles makes your technique more consistent because there is vast potential for movement in your smaller muscles, such as in your wrists and arms. A *scoop* is when you're trying to lift the ball up using your wrists. You want to avoid this move because it creates inconsistent results. I call that shot the "scoopy poopie." You do not want to be a player who has a scoopy poopie in your swing.

Your actual chip shot will also improve, and you know how important the chip shot is during a round of golf. At the 2005 Masters, Tiger Woods was on the par-3, 16th hole, facing a very challenging chip shot. He hit the ball exactly where he planned, toward the high side of the green, and let it trickle down the slope towards the hole. For dramatic effect, the ball paused for a moment on the lip of the hole before falling in. The crowd roared with excitement. It still stands as one of the most famous shots in Masters' history. Woods went on to beat Chris DiMarco with a birdie on the first play-off hole.

The next time you chip the ball into the hole during a round, celebrate like crazy and imagine the roar of the crowd.

So, let's go over your chipping technique. This shot is so easy you can do it with your eyes closed. Literally. Practice with your eyes closed sometimes. It's fun and it builds confidence, too. You learned from Jake and the thousands of members of the International Blind Golf Association, including the US Blind Golf Association, that you can hit all of your shots with your eyes closed. The ball just gets in the way of your swing.

In order for the ball to just get in the way of the pendulum created by your swing, it's important that you are set up correctly. Proper setup is key. Your feet will be close together—about twelve inches apart—and about 70 percent of your weight will be on your lead foot, causing you to lean towards the target.

Relax your shoulders. Your hands will be hanging in front of the inner thigh of your lead leg. When you look at your arms and the shaft of the club, it will look like a lowercase letter *y* or a backward *y*, depending on which side of the ball you are standing on. The club is the stem of the *y*.

Use your upper back and shoulder muscles to swing the *y* back and through in a pendulum motion. Don't let your letter *y* turn into a *V* with a tail. To maintain the *y*, keep your wrists completely still throughout this shot. By keeping your wrists quiet, you will create a simple and repeatable move that will produce more consistent shots.

The key to consistency is the use of your big muscles. Here's a little rhyme to help you remember: Swing the *y* past your thigh! As your back and shoulders initiate the movement and you swing your arms and club back, allow your hands to move past your thigh on both the backswing and the forward swing. You don't want to just keep your hands in front of the middle of your body and move your wrists to swing the club. This technique results in inconsistent shots.

Many of my students instinctively use their wrists to lift, or scoop, the ball up into the air during their chipping technique. Instead, using your big muscles and allowing the club to swing like a pendulum will give you the most consistent technique, which will result in the most consistently successful results. Practicing this way will begin to train the one-piece takeaway for your full swing. If you are finding it challenging to keep your wrists still, try my Professional Anti–Scoopy Poopie grip as a drill. I named it myself.

Here's the drill: Place your lead hand at the bottom of your grip, and then let the grip rest against your forearm. Now, with your trail hand, hold your grip against your forearm. It's like a reverse putting grip with the lead hand lower, but we are adding that you hold the grip against your forearm. Two-time Masters champion Bernhard Langer used to putt with this grip.[17]

This grip may be a little uncomfortable, but it is effective. Practice chipping with this grip and you will be forced to use the big muscles in your upper body to swing your arms and the club back and through.

You can practice your chip shot and one-piece takeaway with the Professional Anti–Scoopy Poopie grip; whether you are at a practice green,

---

17 http://www.pgatour.com/players/player.01666.html

Professional Anti-Scoopy Poopie Grip

in your yard, at a dog park, or at home in a mirror—your entire game will improve. Then, go back to your regular grip, and chip with the goal of using your big muscles and having a repeatable technique and consistent results.

Earlier, I mentioned that practicing your chipping will help improve all parts of your game. You may still be thinking that it's just one shot, and it's only about a quarter of the swing. How can it help the rest of your game? That's a great question.

Practicing chipping will help your putting because when you keep your wrists from scooping and focus on making a pendulum swing with your upper back and shoulders, you are using the same technique that works in putting. The difference with a putting stroke is that you keep your lower body still as well as your wrists. So, gaining trust and confidence in using the bigger upper-body muscles to swing the golf club back and through is essential to having consistency in your game.

In your full swing, consistency comes from using your big muscles to initiate your swing. It's a repeatable move, even in the most stressful situations. Making a shoulder turn is key to the full swing. By practicing the Professional Anti–Scoopy Poopie grip drill, you will feel confident and comfortable using your upper back and shoulders, therefore creating a repeatable move.

Life Consistency

Consistency in life is all about habits and rituals. The more consistently you perform good habits, the more successful you will be.

What is a habit? According to Charles Duhigg, author of *The Power of Habit: Why We Do What We Do in Life and Business*, every habit has three components: There is a cue, a behavior or routine, and a reward. The reward is how our brains learn to encode a pattern for the future.[18]

While reading Duhigg's work, I realized that years ago, when I was the head golf professional at a country club, I had a habit of having a Diet Pepsi every afternoon at about three o'clock. It was like clockwork: I'd suddenly get a craving for a soda. When I analyzed this habit, I understood that the cue was the time of day. My behavior was then to go to the bar and order my soda. You may think the reward was drinking the soda, but it wasn't the soda at all. Going to get the soda allowed me to leave my office and the work that I was doing, walk down the hall and—most importantly for me—talk to people. I would chat with the bartender and anyone sitting at the bar or walking by. As an outgoing person, I gained energy from this socialization. But I thought I was addicted to the soda. Since I don't like to be addicted to anything or to consume unhealthy drinks, I wanted to change this behavior.

Although I didn't fully understand the science and research behind my habit at the time, I knew I needed to do something to interrupt my craving. I started to schedule golf lessons at two-thirty or three o'clock every day. Interacting with clients met my true reward of socialization. I left my office, talked to my staff, and then interacted with my student. I neurologically associated pleasure with socialization; as long as I interacted with people, I no longer craved a Diet Pepsi.

Duhigg says that "40 to 45 percent of what we do every day sort of feels like a decision, but it's actually a habit." What habits would you like to change? What good habits would you like to act on consistently in your day to help you reach your ideal outcome?

What I learned from Tony Robbins, the nation's number one life and business strategist, is that most of our actions are either to gain pleasure or to avoid pain. Therefore, if you would like to change a habit of smoking, poor eating, procrastination, or addiction, you will need to associate pain with the habit and pleasure with a life without the bad habit.

---

18 http://charlesduhigg.com/the-power-of-habit/

Years ago, I was doing Tony's thirty-day cassette program (it was a long time ago) called *Personal Power (Anthony Robbins, Audio Book 1993)*.[19] I was listening to one of the tapes while I was working out. It was about changing a habit. I had not been working out regularly, so I wanted to make a habit of exercising consistently. Tony took me through a meditation where I imagined my life in one year, five years, and ten years if I did *not* exercise regularly. He said to imagine life as bad as it could be, so I pictured feeling tired, unhealthy, and overweight, and I imagined being unable to enjoy activities that I love. I was so deep into the vision that I actually had tears running down my face. I related pain to a habit of not taking care of my physical body. Then he had me do the opposite and I imagined life in one year, five years, ten years—and beyond—being amazing. I pictured looking and feeling fabulous, being healthy, having energy, and feeling such joy as I participated in fun activities with family and friends. That vision of my future was so compelling it gave me the passion to put in the effort to create that life.

The next step was to review that awesome life each day by thinking about my reasons for working out and getting excited about the results. Tony says, "Raise your standards to create lasting change!" Being in shape became my standard. I took that standard to another level in 2014 (about twenty-one years later) after attending a four-day program with Tony Robbins called, "Unleash the Power Within."[20] Tony looks like the Incredible Hulk not only because he stands at six feet seven inches, but also because he is in amazing shape. He truly walks the talk. Since I want to teach and inspire others, I made it a must to be in top physical condition. It takes consistent effort. My habits are working out five days a week and taking a minimum of 10,000 steps every day. When my Fitbit vibrates at 10,000 steps, I celebrate by putting my hands in the air and saying, "I am in the habit of achieving my goals!" I do get a few strange looks when I do my celebration in public! Taking 10,000 steps each day is my habit; it's my standard.

---

19 https://www.amazon.com/Anthony-Robbins-Personal-Power-cassettes/dp/B000GACW28
20 https://www.youtube.com/watch?v=Yl1VXOC3tZU

Consider what have we learned from Charles Duhigg and Tony Robbins, and take some time to think about and analyze habits that you would like to change. Find your cue: Is it the time of day, your location, or the people you are with? Think about when you get a craving or desire, and figure out the situation. Decide what good habits you want to create and set a new standard for yourself.

Write down a habit you want to change.

_____

_____

When do you get the craving or desire? What is the cue?

_____

_____

How will your life be affected if you continue with this bad habit? In one year, what will your life be like? Imagine the worst possible scenario.

_____

_____

_____

_____

_____

In five years, how bad will it be if you continue with your bad habit? What will your life be like?

_____

_____

_____

_____

_____

In ten years, what will your life be like if you keep this bad habit?

_____

_____

_____

_____

Let's replace that old habit with a new awesome habit!
What could you do to alter your habitual response to the cue?

_____

_____

_____

Coach: In this area what coaches, teachers or mentors can you reach out to?
Books I will read:

_____

_____

_____

Videos I will watch:

_____

_____

Audios, like books on tape or podcasts, I will listen to:

_____

_____

Music I will listen to:

_____

_____

_____

Outcome: Be very clear and specific with your new empowering habit.

_____

_____

_____

Reasons: Why do you want to be consistent with this new and better habit?

_____

_____

_____

_____

What will your life be like in one year with this new behavior? What are the positive benefits? Make it as wonderful as you can imagine!

_____

_____

_____

_____

_____

What is your life like in five years with this awesome new standard and habit?

_____

_____

_____

_____

_____

_____

_____

What is your life like in ten years?

_____

_____

_____

_____

_____

_____

_____

Execution: What actions will you consistently take in your life? What is your plan?

_____

_____

_____

_____

_____

Remember to analyze your progress and your plan. If it is not progressing as planned adjust the execution plan, but don't change the goal. You may need to try to do a few things differently.
(The "Tri" in Triumph)

Write down how you will celebrate and reward yourself for consistently performing the new habit.
(The "!" in CORE Triumph!)

_____

_____

_____

_____

_____

Chapter 4: Key Elements

Here are the key elements covered in Chapter 4:

- Use big muscles to make your technique more consistent.
- Practice your chipping technique
  - Keep your wrists still.

- o Swing the letter y back and through like a pendulum.
- o Avoid the scoopy poopie.
- Recognize that many of our actions are habits.
- Know that you are in control of creating the habits and rituals of each day.
- Be consistent with awesome habits to reach your ideal outcomes and set a high standard for your life.

Five

It's a Dance: Move Your Hips

Dance like there's nobody watching,
Love like you'll never be hurt.
Sing like there's nobody listening,
And live like it's heaven on earth.

—William W. Purkey

To me, this quote is saying to live fearlessly and free of doubt. I believe it's also telling us to loosen up and go for it. With this mind-set, you will swing the golf club without tension in your body or skepticism in your mind, as if you are dancing and nobody's watching. In this chapter, you will learn how to keep the rhythm, tempo, and timing consistent for the entire swing. Yes, this is the rhythm-and-groove section of your CORE Triumph! plan. You will also learn some strategies to lower your stress level and increase your confidence—on the golf course and in life.

Coaches	Outcome	Reasons	Execution
• Debbie O'Connell	• Play better golf	• More satisfying rounds of golf	• Read this chapter
• Dr. Herbert Benson	• Less stress in life	• Be more consistent with great shots	• Practice swinging with rhythm
• Amy J. C. Cuddy	• Higher confidence	• Enjoy golf and life every day	• Use thoughts of numbers or generic words to create a consistent swing
	• Happier days	• Succeed in my goals	
		• Feel awesome	• Practice breathing properly
		• Enjoy time with friends and family	• Stand in superhero pose at least two minutes a day to lower stress and gain confidence

Golf is rhythm, tempo, and timing. It's like a rhythmic dance that is executed effortlessly. During this beautiful dance, a small ball gets in the way of the swinging club. The challenge arises when you believe playing golf is about hitting the ball hard with your club.

Here are some definitions of key terms in this chapter:

- *Rhythm* is a repeated pattern of movement.
- *Tempo* is the speed of a motion or activity.
- *Timing* is the plan, schedule, or arrangement of when something should be done.

In the previous chapter, you learned about the takeaway and the backswing. So the dance move is to turn your upper body away from the target and let your arms swing back and up. Your arms will swing up without you feeling as if you are lifting them up. This goes back to the fundamentals of the proper tilt forward, or the tush push, in the setup. With the proper tilt, you are set up to swing the club on an effective swing path.

Once you complete your shoulder turn, it's time to start your forward swing. The next part of your dance move is to lead with your legs and hips. Practice making your dance move *without* a golf club. Maybe even put some music on. This is important because the most effective golf swings have this sequence of moving in the body. Practicing without trying to hit a golf ball will make it easier to move in the proper sequence with good rhythm.

One of my students confidently informed me of her lack of athletic ability the moment we met. I reassured her that golf was not about hand-eye coordination; if it were, there wouldn't be a blind golfers' association. I asked her whether she liked to dance and she said yes. I explained that golf is more about movement and dance than it is about trying to hit a ball. In order to get her moving rhythmically, I put on the song "Bop" by Dan Seals. I instructed her to get into the proper setup position with a golf club and dance. Her move was to turn her shoulders, let her arms swing up, as she felt her weight shift onto her trail leg. The next move she did was to turn toward the target by allowing her weight to shift onto our lead foot, turning her hips towards the target, and allowing our arms to swing down, forward, and then up. Without hesitation, she swung her arms down and repeated the move. We had a great time dancing together! My student was able to feel the rhythm, tempo, and timing of a golf swing.

I love to dance. You may not even *like* to dance, but I'm sure you can count. One of my students was struggling with the rhythm and tempo of his golf swing. He would put the rhythm, tempo, and timing of his golf swing together sometimes, but repeating the successful shot was truly a challenge. To help him maintain a repeatable tempo, I had him count in his head during the swing. He is an exceptional pianist, so counting was easy for him. He would actually count in terms of whole, half, and quarter notes, which was familiar and comfortable for him. His count for the full swing was *one, two, three* during the backswing, and *four* while he swung forward to the finish. The counting made his rhythm very consistent.

We changed the count for his half swing and pitch shot to *one, two* during the backswing and *three* during his forward swing—a waltz tempo. His chip shot was simply *one* (back) and then *two* (through).

Counting in your mind as you swing will improve your swing in a few key ways. First, it will help you keep consistent rhythm, tempo, and timing, as we discussed. The other core ingredient to successful repeatable execution on the golf course is to keep your mind from thinking mechanically about a specific movement of a body part or dwelling on negative thoughts. When you put numbers in your mind, you keep out any thoughts that could get in the way of your rhythmic swing.

The next time you go out to the practice area, try counting during your swings. If counting isn't comfortable, use words. One of my students said "peanut butter" for her full swing. I learned the words "super fluid" from an awesome book called *Quantum Golf* (Enhanger and Wallace 1991). We are all different. Find the words or numbers or whatever else is the best way for you to quiet your mind and maintain your rhythm.

The key to having consistent rhythm, tempo, and timing is to release the tension from your body. The acceleration of your arms and the clubhead through impact is a result of the movement of your core, not because you tighten or stress your muscles. You want to feel *effortless power,* not *powerless effort.*

A comment I hear from many of my students is, "I work so hard, but the ball doesn't go anywhere!" Then I hear about their frustration levels rising during a round of golf.

I'm sure you've made this swing before. I call it the "I Don't Give a Hoot" swing. It usually happens when you are not in a tournament. You hit a few shots that are not up to par and you feel frustrated. Then it happens—another poor shot is the last straw—so, in frustration, you throw a ball on the ground and just swing at it. The swing is effortless, the ball flies beautifully, and you are balanced. You immediately ask, "Why don't I hit them like that all the time?" The reason is that you care too much and try too hard on most shots.

In order to become tension free, just before you swing take one last look at the target and breathe in. Then as you look back at the ball, slowly breathe out. At the completion of your exhale begin your swing.

I have two awesome and very simple methods to reduce stress and anxiety on the golf course and in everyday life.

1. Breathe

Yes, breathe, but breathe deeply. According to the Better Health Channel, "When a person is under stress, their breathing pattern changes. Typically, an anxious person takes small, shallow breaths, using their shoulders rather than their diaphragm to move air in and out of their lungs. This style of breathing disrupts the balance of gases in the body."[21]

Shallow overbreathing, or hyperventilation, can prolong feelings of anxiety by making the physical symptoms of stress worse. Controlling your breathing can help to improve some of these symptoms.

If you are not paying attention to your breathing, you may be inadvertently prolonging stress with shallow breaths, making it harder to release tension and execute great golf shots.

There is a solution. Dr. Herbert Benson discovered something that he termed "the relaxation response." He is a cardiologist and a professor of mind-body medicine at Harvard Medical School.[22]

The relaxation response is a physical state of deep rest that changes the physical and emotional responses to stress. For example, it decreases heart rate, blood pressure, rate of breathing, and reduces muscle tension. You don't have to take a nap on the golf course to elicit the response. The American Institute of Stress (AIS) recommends using deep breathing to evoke the relaxation response. "Deep breathing increases the supply of oxygen to your brain

---

21 https://www.betterhealth.vic.gov.au/health/healthyliving/breathing-to-reduce-stress
22 https://www.bensonhenryinstitute.org/about/dr-Herbert-benson

and stimulates the parasympathetic nervous system, which promotes a state of calmness."[23] Now, calmness and golf go together well.

I'm sure you have seen many athletes during a competition take a deep breath before a big shot or a major play. It works.

According to Harvard Medical School health publications,[24] this is how effective deep breathing works:

1. Breathe in slowly and deeply, pushing your stomach out so that your diaphragm is put to maximum use.
2. Hold your breath briefly.
3. Exhale slowly, thinking R-E-L-A-X as your belly deflates, once again putting your diaphragm to maximal use.
4. Repeat the entire sequence five to ten times, concentrating on breathing deeply and slowly.

Abdominal breathing is when your belly goes out as you breathe in, as if there is a balloon in your belly that is blown up when you inhale. When you breathe out, your belly deflates. Practice proper breathing. It will come in handy when you are feeling anxious on or off the golf course.

2. Posture

Proper posture can reduce stress and increase confidence. Your mother probably told you to stand up straight. Well, she was giving you great advice. According to Amy J. C. Cuddy, an associate professor at Harvard Business School, positioning your body in a power pose can increase your testosterone level (a hormone that increases confidence and power) and lower your level of cortisol (a stress hormone).[25]

My favorite power pose is to stand like a superhero. There is a reason our superheroes stand tall with their hands on their hips, their chests out and chins up, and their weight evenly balanced. For the gentlemen, I call it the Superman

---

23 http://www.stress.org/take-a-deep-breath/

24 http://www.askdoctork.com/how-do-breathing-exercises-work-to-relieve-stress-201211083638

25 http://www.ted.com/talks/amy_cuddy_your_body_language_shapes_who_you_are

pose and, for the women, I call it the Wonder Woman pose. Within two minutes of standing in your superhero pose, you will change your levels of testosterone and cortisol.

One day, I was playing a round of golf and my playing partner was really struggling. I gave her a few words of advice, such as to loosen her grip and relax, but she was getting so frustrated that she caused tension in her body. After a triple bogey, she looked at me and said, "What should I do?" I told her to stand like Wonder Woman. She gave me a look of disbelief. My guess is that she was thinking, "You are a golf professional, and I need some advice on my game!" I went to tee off on the next hole—a par-3—and she stood by the cart in the powerful Wonder Woman pose. I intentionally took my time so she could stand in her pose long enough to make a change in her body. The result was a par on the next hole, then bogey, par, and par. She was thrilled. "Wow! That really worked!" she said.

To reduce stress on the golf course or anywhere else throughout the day, stand in your power pose, and take slow deep breaths that let your diaphragm inflate. You will feel confident and fearless. The key benefit to your golf game is that you will be more relaxed as you swing and have better rhythm, tempo, and timing in all of your shots. When you reduce stress, you will be able to perform measurably better in activities, presentations, and more.

I think the most important aspect of this chapter is for you to understand that you are in charge—of your thoughts, your emotions, and even your hormone levels. Take charge and enjoy every day.

When I have a speech to give, I want to be sure that I am in a peak state to give my best to the audience. I stand in my Wonder Woman pose and take deep breaths for at least two minutes before it's time to start.

Part of the research performed by Amy J. C. Cuddy and her team included an interview process. Half of the interviewees stood with their arms crossed and their heads down just before the interview. The other half stood in a power pose. A group of people watched the interviews, not knowing about the poses performed. When the observers were asked whom they would hire, 100 percent of the people chosen were those who had been standing in the power pose.

Any time you have an important meeting, presentation, speech, test, task, or event where you want to feel powerful and confident, take two minutes, and stand in the power pose. You will perform measurably better.

During one of my corporate outings, a participant shared a story with the group about a meeting where she was the only woman of the twelve people at the table. Each time she attempted to join in the conversation and share her thoughts and opinions, she was interrupted or ignored. She was getting very frustrated. At that moment, she remembered Amy J. C. Cuddy's TED talk on power posing. Although she was uncomfortable with the position, she leaned back in her chair, put her hands behind her head, and sat quietly. Within a minute of changing her posture, she was asked a question and had the room's undivided attention.

You are in charge of your thoughts, feelings, and hormones! Use these skills to make all of the events and challenges in your life even better. Your days will be filled with great rhythm, tempo, and timing, and they will feel effortless. You'll have the confidence to dance and not care whether anyone is watching.

What are your reasons for taking charge of your emotions and hormone levels throughout the day? What areas of your golf game and your life could be even better with less stress and more confidence?

_____

_____

_____

_____

What is your execution plan? Some examples could include practicing deep breathing or standing in a power pose. Be specific about when you will perform these actions.

_____

_____

_____

_____

Chapter 5: Key Elements

Here are the key elements covered in Chapter 5:

- Release tension in your body so you can swing with effective rhythm, tempo, and timing.
- Take deep breaths and stand in a power pose for at least two minutes to lower stress levels.
- Include a deep breath in your pre-shot routine.
- Know that you are in charge of your thoughts, feelings, and hormones (both testosterone and cortisol).
- Remember that you have the skills to live a more confident, stress-free life.

Six

Impact

Everything you do has some effect, some impact.

—Dalai Lama

In this chapter, we will develop your CORE Triumph! strategy for impact. I will focus on your understanding of impact and its effect on ball flight. There are some effective drills for you to make your impact position even better. Finally, we will examine the impact you are making in life.

Coaches
- Debbie O'Connell
- Oprah Winfrey

Outcome
- Hit the ball more solidly
- Hit the ball at the intended target
- Make a positive impact in life
- Leave a legacy

Reasons
- Play better golf
- Swing confidently
- Enjoy the game more
- Feel awesome
- Bring joy to others

Execution
- Read this chapter
- Practice the suggested drills indoors and outdoors
- Complete the CORE Triumph! exercise at the end of the chapter to define your plan for creating a legacy

Impact is that fraction of a second when the clubface makes contact with the golf ball. It is the moment of truth. There are three core components that affect the direction your golf ball will travel: the direction the clubface is aiming, the path the club is traveling and the angle the clubhead approaches the ball. In this chapter, we will focus mainly on the clubface position at impact, which controls 70 percent of the direction the ball will travel.

During the full swing, you want to have a solid lead wrist and a forward-shaft lean at impact to experience the best contact at the moment of truth. The forward-shaft lean means your hands and the handle of the club are ahead of the clubhead at the moment you make contact with the golf ball. In Chapter 4, I suggested you practice the Professional Anti–Scoopy Poopie grip drill to prevent you from attempting to scoop or lift the ball up into the air. This drill will help to create the forward-shaft lean and solid impact position during your full swing, as well.

By now, I'm confident you have practiced and improved your impact position in your chip shot. So, let's get to the next step. Make a half swing, still focusing on hitting the ball low by keeping your hands ahead of the club-head through impact. You may be asking where the power comes from since you used to hit the ball hard with your wrists at impact. Well, that was the problem.

Impact

It's quite a challenge to have consistently perfect timing at impact using your wrists. That is often the reason you may top the ball or hit the ground just before the ball. Also, as your wrist muscles attempt to strike the ball, more loft is created in the clubhead at impact. More loft results in a higher, shorter shot.

You have already learned how to use your big muscles, so let's make sure that a scoop at impact is not getting in the way of power and consistency.

After a number of half swings—both at the golf course and in front of the mirror at home—you are ready for your full swing. Begin with a 9-iron at medium speed, and focus on maintaining the same solid feeling at impact as you felt in the half swings. You can visualize hitting the ball with the back of your lead hand to help you maintain the forward shaft lean. Once you are hitting the ball solidly at that speed, go to 75 percent for a few swings, and then go to your regular tempo.

A great way to improve your position at impact is to practice hitting low shots. You can either use your imagination or bring a swimming noodle to your practice session. Put the noodle about ten feet in front of you, horizontally, but about three feet above the ground. I put a couple of golf club shafts from broken clubs or alignment sticks, which can be purchased at most golf stores, at each end and securely place them in the ground and through the ends of the noodle. Hit the ball under the noodle. You can start it higher off the ground in the beginning and then lower it as you improve this low shot. In order to be successful with this low shot, keep your hands in front of the golf ball at impact, creating the forward shaft lean!

This drill will improve your alignment, as well as your position at impact. To successfully hit low, solid shots, your lead wrist must be firm, and your hands must be ahead of the ball at impact with an extended lead arm. Attention to your alignment is also a core ingredient to hitting the ball directly under the noodle. This is a challenging way to practice. And it's fun. It will also give you confidence to hit the ball low, maybe under a tree on the golf course.

In addition to practicing at the driving range (and especially if you don't have time to get to the driving range), make some slow-motion swings in front of a mirror. Take a moment to check your fundamentals. Start your takeaway with your shoulders, arms, hands, and club all moving together in your one-piece move, the big muscles turning and letting the club swing to the top of the backswing. When you get back to impact, you want the clubface square to the target, with your hands still ahead of the clubhead at impact. This is the forward-shaft lean that I mentioned earlier. Go ahead and swing to the finish. Practice this slow-motion swing a couple times a week for about ten minutes per session. It will make a huge difference on the ball at impact. It will also eliminate the scoopy poopie.

Now that you are in a solid position at impact, it's time to make sure the clubface is square to your target at impact. I have a couple of great drills for you to practice your release, but let me explain the release first. The release is a rotation of your forearms and wrists by turning the back of your lead wrist toward the ground. It's the opposite of a scoop. As we know, the back of the lead wrist is firm through impact, but we do want it to rotate. This rotation not only squares up the clubface, it also creates more clubhead speed.

The first drill I want you to do is without a golf club. I call it the Hitchhiker Drill. In your setup, let your lead arm hang down, and fold your fingers in, but point your thumb out and away from you. Now, begin your backswing: Turn your shoulder and swing your arm up until it is parallel to the ground, with your thumb now pointing toward the sky (*photo 1*). Start your forward move by rotating your body and swinging your arm back toward impact. Rotate your forearm so your thumb returns to its starting position, and then continue to rotate your body and arm until your thumb is pointing toward the sky on the target side of your body (*photo 2*).

Photo 1

Photo 2

Now, make the same move with a golf club in your hand. Make a half swing back so the toe of your club (the part of the clubhead that is the farthest away from you in your setup) is pointing toward the sky, swing through impact with a square clubface and then toward the target. Finish the half swing with the toe up again. Make this swing back and forth without stopping and as fast as you can to improve the speed in which you square the face. This is important because most golfers slice the ball by having an open clubface at impact. So, if you practice squaring up the clubface quickly, you will eliminate your slice. Practice hitting golf balls with this drill and feel how your forearms and wrists rotate through impact.

The other drill that I have found incredibly successful is to make a golf swing standing straight up, as if the ball were waist high. It's a Baseball-Swing Drill. When you make this swing, you want to hear a *whoosh* sound at the imaginary impact location and just after (*photo 3*). Again, feel your arms rotate. I found standing up and swinging in this position makes it easier to rotate your forearms through impact.

You now have all of the core ingredients to make solid contact with a square clubface at impact. Please do not think of all of this while you are playing. It's too much to think about when impact happens so quickly. Even in the practice area, after your drills, you want to make swings where you turn off all thoughts about your swing, engage a target, and swing effortlessly. I love drills to help you improve, but then it's time to play.

I played college basketball and we did many drills in practice to improve our fundamentals. When the whistle blew and the ball was tossed in the air, I did not think about how to make a chest pass or how to bend my knees to shoot the ball or how to make the lay-up; I just played. That's what you want to do on the golf course. Remembering the difference between the *Think Box* and the *Play Box* will be a positive impact on your golf game.

Once you have improved your understanding of impact, you will have a lot more fun on the golf course. The same is true in life. The happiest people are often the ones who are making a positive impact on other people.

Your Impact in Life

What kind of impact are you making in life? One of Oprah Winfrey's favorite sayings is, "Please take responsibility for the energy that you bring into this space."[26] Do you brighten the room when you walk into it? Take a moment and think about how you impact other people.

One day after work, a friend and I went to a restaurant to have a cocktail and dinner. We decided to sit at the bar. The bartender was not in a very friendly mood that day. She didn't smile at all. She was very matter of fact. Her attitude was surprising, considering that she was in the service business and that her tip amount was undecided at that point. I figured we had a choice: Get upset that the bartender was not friendly, ignore her completely, or make a positive impact. I turned to my friend, who was also disappointed with our interaction with the bartender, and said, "I bet you a drink that I can make her smile before you can." She agreed.

When the bartender returned to deliver our beverages my friend jumped right in with her attempt to elicit a smile. Well, she just crashed. It wasn't even close. We laughed at the failed attempt. The bartender returned to take our dinner order and I had my goal, my reasons, and my plan in mind. I asked the bartender for some recommendations. I figured if I could get her talking a little, she might loosen up. Then I asked how the turkey burger tasted. She said, "It's very good; it's my favorite," but she said it without a smile. My reaction was so upbeat and enthusiastic about how much I loved turkey burgers and how thrilled I was by her recommendation that she couldn't help but smile. Free beer came my way. But, truly, our competition to make the bartender smile was more than winning a drink. Our entire dining experience was so much better because of the complete change in the bartender's attitude and energy. I'm confident my friend and I made an impact on her night at work by using CORE Triumph! We achieved our outcome—to get the bartender to smile—and our reasons were to make our experience more pleasant as well as to make a positive impact on her night, and we executed the plan. The next time you have the opportunity to change someone's mood, go for it, and make a positive impact.

---

26 http://www.kimvazquez.com/like-oprah-said-your-energy-matters.html

Another time I encountered an individual who was not smiling and did not appear to be very happy with her job was in a casino while playing black-jack. The dealer looked and acted like someone who was having a very bad day. I offered the challenge of who could make the dealer smile first to my friends and admitted that this could be a tough one. The drinks were free, so only the tip was at stake, but we were all competitive and wanted to be the person to make the dealer smile. We also knew that positive energy at a blackjack table could make a difference in our finances. I'm not sure how that works in gambling, but it seems as if the energy at the table affects the cards. As each of us put forth an effort to create a moment of joy in our dealer's life, we realized the difficulty of the task. She was tough to break. But then, the camaraderie of all the female players kicked in, and some personal talk brought out a chuckle and a smile. Once she cracked, she laughed along and talked with us for the rest of her shift. I didn't win the competition, but we all won, both with the cards and making an impact on the dealer's night. We also had a blast.

What kind of impact do you make on others? What kind of impact would you like to make? Maybe you feel it's not your responsibility to make others happy. Maybe you believe that happiness comes from within and we all need to find it for ourselves. In life, we cannot help but interact with others. You will make a positive, negative, or neutral impact during any interaction, whether it's on social media or in person. You can choose the impact you leave. You can also decide on the legacy you would like to leave in life.

Imagine for a moment that you are at the end of your life. Picture the life you have led and the impact you've made. What is your legacy? What was the meaning or purpose of your life? Are you happy with what you see? If not, then start now to make your impact. Your impact can change the world or enlighten a few people—you choose.

We all know of the legacies (some positive and some negative) of many historic figures, including our presidents. Many have a legacy making a significant and positive impact on the world: Albert Einstein, Martin Luther King, Jr., Jackie Robinson, Eleanor Roosevelt, Susan B. Anthony, Mother Teresa, Rosa Parks, Mahatma Gandhi, Nelson Mandela, Alexander Graham Bell,

Jonas Salk, the Wright brothers, Henry Ford, Bill Gates, and Oprah Winfrey. The list could go on for pages.

Many children and young adults are already creating their legacies:

- Zach Bonner, an advocate for homeless youth, walked 2,300 miles across America to raise awareness. He founded the Little Red Wagon Foundation when he was seven years old. Zach received the Presidential Service Award in 2006.
- When Ana Dodson was eleven years old, she started Peruvian Hearts to support children in Peru, her native country. She was adopted when she was three and grew up in the United States.
- Ashley Shuyler was sixteen years old when she founded AfricAid—an organization focused on improving girls' education in Africa. She has raised nearly $700,000 to support these efforts.
- Young Emily Lopez was eight when she decided to raise money for autism research after seeing the effect of Asperger syndrome on her brother. She set up lemonade stands – "Lemonade 4 Autism" – and 100 percent of the money she receives is donated to charity.
- Bilaal Rajan was named an official United Nations International Children's Emergency Fund (UNICEF) ambassador at age eight. He has raised money for dozens of causes, including disaster relief, HIV and AIDS orphans, and schools for impoverished communities. To raise awareness of underprivileged youth, Bilaal goes barefoot each year for National Volunteer Week.

There are other ways to leave a legacy, as well. Make an impact in your own family by spending time together and teaching children things like riding a bicycle, swimming, playing golf, playing an instrument, or anything that will serve them well in life. Give to charity or volunteer your time. By making a positive impact on those around you, you are leaving a legacy of inspiration, happiness, and generosity.

A legacy doesn't happen by accident. It takes thought and planning. To leave a legacy and make an impact, go through CORE Triumph!

Coach: Who is your coach or mentor? How does that person inspire you?

_____
_____
_____

Outcome: What will your legacy be? Whom will you impact?

_____
_____
_____

Reasons: Why is this important to you?

_____
_____
_____

Execution: Write a plan, and take action.

_____
_____
_____

Chapter 6: Key Elements

Here are the key elements covered in Chapter 6:

- Improve the position of the clubface at impact because it controls 70 percent of the direction the golf ball travels.
- Practice chip shots and half swings with a focus on keeping your hands ahead of the clubhead at impact.
- Practice your release.
- Take time to think about the impact you make on others.
- Decide on the legacy you want to leave.

Seven

Ambition is the path to success. Persistence
is the vehicle you arrive in.

—Bill Bradley

In this chapter, we will examine swing path—the path in which your club travels during your swing—and teach you drills to get you on an even better path. We will also examine the limiting beliefs that may be affecting your golf success and ideal path for your life. So, let's develop the CORE Triumph! plan for your path.

Coaches	Outcome	Reasons	Execution
• Debbie O'Connell	• Improve swing	• Make better golf shots	• Read this chapter
• Dr. Matthew B. James, MA, PhD	• Improve swing path	• Get lower scores	• Do the swing-path drills
• Michael Breed	• Get on desired path in life	• Have more fun on the golf course	• Answer all of the questions in this chapter
		• Be happier	

The path that your clubhead is traveling as it approaches impact is a contributing factor to the direction that your ball will fly. As I mentioned in Chapter 6, the clubface position at impact determines about 70 percent of the ball's direction, but the swing path is very important as well.

Before I explain the simplest and most effective swing path for most golfers, I want you to know that you do not have to have a perfect swing path to be successful. Nancy Lopez's first move to start her backswing is to lift her hands and then her club travels inside of the typically straight back path of a golf club. Basically, the clubhead goes behind her. I tell my students all the time not to swing around their "assets" (their backsides) because the swing is more difficult, but that's not true for Nancy. Then, Nancy lifts her arms, gets the club in position at the top of her backswing and has a perfect path through impact. The rest is history—she has forty-eight wins on the LPGA Tour, and has been inducted into the LPGA Tour and World Golf Halls of Fame.

Another player with an untraditional swing path is PGA Tour professional Jim Furyk. Jim takes the club straight back which, in the golf industry, is considered on a good path. As he begins his forward swing, he drops the club inside of where a typically desired swing would go and he lays the clubhead back behind him. This move would make it impossible for most golfers to hit the ball well, but Jim's position at impact is awesome. He has twenty-seven professional wins and a U.S. Open trophy. In 2016, he shot the lowest score ever on the PGA Tour, a 58. I'd say his swing path is perfect for him!

I mention both Nancy and Jim because I want you to understand you can swing the club in a variety of ways and still be very successful. Having said that, through research and years of studying the best golfers, there is a path of least resistance, meaning there is an easier way to swing the club and hit more golf shots in the desired direction.

If you have been playing golf for years and your path is not classic—but it's consistent—and you get to a great position at the top of your swing and, more importantly, at impact, then you may not want to change it. But if your swing path is all over the place, making your shots inconsistent, then let's get to work.

When I'm giving a lesson and videotaping my student's swing from a down the target line position, I will make two lines: One along the shaft of the club that continues past my student's body and another from the ball to the student's shoulder. The goal is to swing the clubhead between those two lines on both the backswing and the forward swing.

The golf swing is a circular motion. It's not a merry-go-round or a Ferris wheel; it's somewhere in between. This in-between circle is called the swing plane. Imagine that there is a big red marker on the end of your golf club and, when you make your golf swing, it will draw a circle.

Now that you can visualize the proper path, let's get you to feel an effective swing path. Make a few golf swings standing straight up, as if the golf ball is at chest height (*see Chapter 6*). The swing plane in this drill is like that of a baseball swing: It's a true circular motion. Feel how you rotate your upper back and allow your hips and body to turn forward. For the next swing, begin your forward tilt so you change the swing plane. Then on your third swing, tilt a little more, again changing your swing plane. Finally, start in your regular golf setup with your full tilt. Feel the same rotation back and through in your body as you felt when you were standing straight up. It's still a circular motion, but now you're on a different plane.

I want you to feel the club swing back and up to the top of your swing. It's truly a golf swing, both back and through to the finish. You don't need to lift the club up with your arms. Just let them swing up as a result of your upper body's turn.

As a teacher, I've had many students whose goal was to avoid hitting a slice. During one of my lessons on this subject, I had my student go from slicing the ball to hooking it about ten minutes into the lesson. I was thrilled. We changed his ball flight by changing the shape of his swing and the position of his clubface at impact. He looked at me, very confused by my enthusiasm, and said, "But now I'm hooking it!"

I replied, "Well, you didn't say that you didn't want to hook it. You just said you didn't want to slice it anymore!" After his jaw dropped, I laughed and reassured him that he would be hitting a nice draw by the end of the lesson, and he was.

To make a change in your swing, you may have to experience the opposite exaggeration of the current move that you are doing incorrectly.

A slice is usually caused by an over-the-top move. That means if we trace the path of your club, it will be above the swing plane line on its way toward the ball. The path of your clubhead as it approaches impact is outside the target line and then moves inside the target line immediately after impact.

Over-the-top downswing move

I have two great drills to get you on the right swing path:

- **Drop Drill**: Swing back about three-quarters of the way and stop. At this point, keep your body still, and let your arms and the club just

73

drop. Literally, let gravity pull your arms and the club straight down to the ground. You'll hear a thud as the clubhead lands on the ground near your back foot.

After doing the drop with your body staying still three times, you're going to actually hit the ball. Start by making the same backswing, but this time, start the lower-body move by turning your hips toward the target and shifting your weight toward the target as your arms are dropping. The club will drop into the perfect swing path for a great shot.

- **Dice Drill**: Line up five golf balls as they would look on a die with five dots. You will be hitting the ball that's in the middle. If you are working on getting rid of a slice, remove the golf ball at the inside back corner and the one at the outside far corner. Now, your die shows three dots. Make your swing and hit only the middle golf ball. This will create an inside-to-outside path through impact. Look at the divots your golf club creates on the ground to see the direction of your swing path. If your challenge is a path that is too far from the inside to the outside, then remove the other two golf balls from the five, and swing on a more outside-to-inside path through impact. You will get immediate feedback about your swing path. This drill comes from Michael Breed, host of *The Golf Fix* on the Golf Channel.

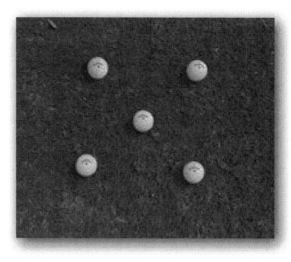

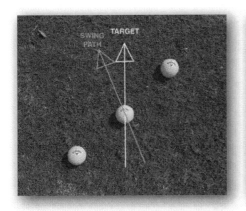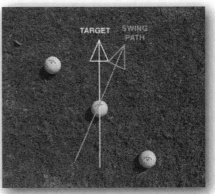

Being on a good path in golf will certainly help get you to your target. There's a parallel in life.

Your Path in Life

Are you on the right path in life? Will the path you are walking lead you to an amazing life of joy and fulfillment? If your answer is yes, awesome. Good for you. Keep going on that path. If it's not, ask yourself, "Why am I on this path when it's not leading me in the direction of my ideal outcome?" Or maybe you were on the path but somehow were knocked off of it.

What is stopping you from getting on the yellow brick road to ultimate happiness? As we found out in *The Wizard of Oz*, the limiting beliefs of the Lion, the Scarecrow, the Tin Man, and Dorothy kept them from attaining the lives they dreamed of. Although the Wizard was a disappointment, they each learned that the thing they were searching for was inside them all along. They just didn't believe it.

Let's take some time to examine some of your beliefs. You may be sabotaging yourself because of the lies your subconscious mind still believes. A limiting belief is a false belief that appears to be true. These beliefs are acquired through life experiences, other people's comments, media, movies, television shows, and more. Here are some examples of limiting beliefs that may be knocking you off your path:

- I'm not smart enough.
- Nobody likes the person who is the best.
- I'm not good enough.
- I'm lazy.
- I'm not athletic, so I'll never be a good golfer.
- I can't be honest because others will judge me harshly.
- I can't love anyone because I will get my heart broken.
- I can't trust anyone because people will hurt me.
- I'm a failure.
- I don't have the resources to succeed.
- I don't have enough time.
- I don't deserve to be successful.

And here are some of the limiting beliefs we learn as children:

- Money is the root of all evil.
- Money doesn't grow on trees.
- Boys don't cry.
- Entrepreneurs are sleazy.
- Bad things happen to good people.
- Nobody likes the winner.
- Nobody likes a loser.

Do any of these false and limiting beliefs ring a bell for you? Don't worry. You can change your limiting beliefs. The first step is to recognize the false belief. So if you have already identified at least one, we are off to a great start. If not, dig a little deeper. Look at areas of your life that are not fulfilling or satisfying your desires and expectations. Then, examine your beliefs.

Ever since I was in my late teens, I have been interested in understanding myself and knowing my true being from the core. I attended at least four Silva Mind Control seminars between ages eighteen and twenty-two, took a class on neuro-linguistic programming (NLP), did a ropes course (which was fantastic), and attended a workshop called "A Course in Miracles." I desired to learn and grow as a person—to be the best I could be. I continued reading positive motivating books and listening to recordings of great speakers, such as Norman Vincent Peale, Zig Ziglar, Tony Robbins, and more. All of this education gave me a better understanding of myself and helped me to become a better teacher by realizing that often in life, we get in our own way because of beliefs that are simply untrue.

When I'm asked about my teaching philosophy, I explain I help people get out of their own way. One of my students was so hard on herself during our lessons. Even when she hit a very good shot, she made a negative comment. It was almost automatic for her to find fault with herself and her golf game. I decided to find an area of her life where she felt confident and believed in her abilities. When I asked her to tell me about something in her life that she felt good about, she shared she was a nationally ranked chess player. As soon as she started talking about chess, her face brightened, her energy level sky-rocketed, and her body language completely changed as she stood taller with her chin up. It was an amazing transformation. I commented on how much belief and confidence she had when she talked about chess, which was very different from all of the other subjects (including golf) that we had discussed. She completely opened up to me and explained that her dad was constantly critical of her and told her she never did anything right. It was so sad to hear about her upbringing and to realize she had carried these false beliefs around for her entire life. I had tears in my eyes.

I asked whether she believed what her dad told her about herself. She hesitated and said, "No, but it's hard to change." We talked more about chess and the qualities of a nationally ranked chess player, which included intelligence, thoughtfulness, an ability to strategize, confidence, and intuition. I reminded her that those qualities were hers twenty-four hours a day—they were part of her makeup.

When we started to hit golf balls again, I made her say something positive about every shot. If the shot was really poor, she would say, "I can do better!" She started to hit better shots. Our wrap-up of the lesson was more about understanding her beliefs and getting rid of the ones that were simply untrue. I encouraged her to replace those limiting beliefs with empowering beliefs, as we just had done during the golf lesson. Thinking about her exceptional chess playing skills was one way to help her come up with empowering beliefs.

Often during a lesson, students share very personal stories of heartache or tragedy. With those stories, we find limiting beliefs that are affecting not only their golf successes but also their happiness life.

What are your roadblocks? Think about your core beliefs and then ask yourself whether they truly make sense. Matthew B. James, MA, PhD, offers some steps you can take to get started on a path of empowering beliefs and a more fulfilling, happier life:[27]

- **Step One**: Write down your limiting beliefs. Play detective, and follow your thoughts and emotions to discover the limiting beliefs that hold you back. Put them on paper and stare them in the face. You might note how strong each belief is and which emotions each elicits in you.
- **Step Two**: Acknowledge that these are beliefs, not truths. This is often the hardest step, but it's the place where choice comes in. Which are you more interested in—defending your limitations to the death or achieving your goals and desires? As author Evelyn Waugh wrote, "When we argue for our limitations, we get to keep them." You choose.
- **Step Three**: Try on a different belief. Use your imagination and try on a belief that is aligned with what you want. It might be something like, "My financial difficulties in the past have taught me so much that I'm fully prepared to handle them now." Or you may tell yourself, "Now that I've been in an unhealthy relationship, I've learned what to look for in a happy, loving partner!"

  The trick is to go beyond just saying it. You want to really step into this new belief and feel how it feels. Done thoroughly, Steps Two and Three will go a long way toward dismantling your old limiting decisions.

---

27 https://www.psychologytoday.com/blog/focus-forgiveness/201311/4-steps-release-limiting-beliefs-learned-childhood

- **Step Four**: Take different actions. This might feel scary, but act as if your new belief is true. In other words, if you really are the kind of man whom women adore, how will you act at parties? Whom might you ask out? If you really are financially successful and have learned a tremendous amount from your past financial difficulties, what steps will you take? If you really are the kind of person who eats healthy food, what will you put in your grocery cart?

Let's do this!

Write down two limiting beliefs that are affecting your golf game or your life.

_____

_____

Acknowledge that these are just beliefs, not truths. Give an example of a real life experience that proves the limiting (false) belief to be untrue.

_____

_____

_____

_____

_____

Write down two empowering beliefs to replace the old false beliefs.

_____

_____

Now, it's time for CORE Triumph! As Dr. James says, "Take a different action."

Coach: Who is the *coach* or mentor you will engage?

_____

Outcome: How will you act or think differently with this new empowering belief?

_____
_____
_____
_____

Reasons: Why do you want to have this new belief and take new actions in your life?

_____
_____
_____
_____
_____

Execution: What steps will you take to *execute* your CORE Triumph! strategy to get on a better path?

_____
_____
_____
_____
_____

Chapter 7: Key Elements

Here are the key elements covered in Chapter 7:

- There is no single swing path that is perfect for every golfer.
- You can make your swing path better and more consistent with a few drills: Baseball-Swing Drill, Drop Drill, Michael Breed's Dice Drill.

- You should think about the path you are on in life. Is it the path to your ideal outcome?
- You should think about any limiting beliefs that are keeping you from achieving your goals.
- You can change your false beliefs into empowering beliefs.

Eight

I can give you a six-word formula for success:
Think things through—then follow through.

—Eddie Rickenbacker

Your CORE Triumph! plan for this chapter is to follow through. You will learn how to get to a perfectly balanced finish position with great follow through in your golf swing. You'll also get started and be motivated to follow through on a personal goal. Let's get started and then follow through.

Coaches	Outcome	Reasons	Execution
• Debbie O'Connell • Ben Hogan	• The ability to have an effective follow-through in golf and life • Complete tasks in life	• More consistent good shots • Lower scores • More fun playing golf • A feeling of accomplishment in life • Improved life • Happier feelings	• Read this chapter • Do the suggested drills • Think the word "finish" on the golf course • Write down your outcome, reasons, and execution plans for a life goal • Follow through with the execution plan

Follow through. Let me write that again. *Follow through.* Wow. Those are very powerful words because to me, they say success. What do they mean? The definition of follow through is "the act of continuing a plan, project, scheme, or the like to its completion."[28] Follow through is key to success in life, career, relationships, athletics, and golf swings.

You may be wondering why the follow-through in golf is important when the ball has already been hit. Or, maybe, you fall back from the target in your finish position; you've tried for years to transfer your weight onto your forward foot to a proper finish, so you're ready to give up on the perfect finish. Whatever you do, I've seen worse, and the great news is that we can make your

---

28 http://www.dictionary.com/browse/follow--through?s=t

follow-through even better. The result will be more powerful and straighter golf shots. You can do it.

The first key to an even better follow-through is understanding and completely accepting that the ball is not the target. You may ask, "What? I'm trying to hit the golf ball. Why is that not my target?" Your target is where you want the ball to go, such as the flag or an object that is in line with the center of the fairway.

Your goal is not to hit the golf ball. It is to make a golf swing with rhythm, tempo, and timing all the way to a balanced finish position. The ball is just in the way.

It's important to follow through—to keep the club moving through impact to your finish—in all golf shots. Your finish position will vary for the different shots in golf, but for all shots, you'll want to follow through to the finish because you will make the best contact with the ball through impact. For this chapter, we are going to focus on the finish position for your full swing.

Most likely, you've seen LPGA Tour professional Michelle Wie hit a driver. She creates so much clubhead speed with the momentum of the club and the rotation of her body that the clubhead follows through so far it is pointing toward the target in the finish. Her upper body rotates through so fully that her chest is facing the gallery that was behind her during her setup. That's also a result of youth, flexibility, and fearlessness. PGA Tour professional Rickie Fowler has a similar finish position. So you may not be able to finish exactly like Michelle or Rickie, but the idea is that you will have so much momentum, the only reason your golf club and arms stop swinging is because they are attached to your body. You'll actually feel a false sense of being a bit out of control, but as long as you are balanced, you'll be fine.

A finish position that resembles a professional golfer's will have great balance and full body rotation toward the target and beyond. Professionals making a full swing do not stop immediately after impact because they have so much momentum and acceleration that they have to keep going. I'm going to share with you the keys to a great follow-through and finish and how to make it automatic.

You might be thinking, "I already look like a professional in my finish position." That is awesome. Reading this chapter will give you proven strategies to make sure you continue your great technique. Or you may be wondering whether this is possible because you've tried to get to a better finish for years. Yes. You can do this. I know because I've taught thousands of golfers to make an effortless, yet powerful, swing. When you follow through to a great finish position with perfect balance, something good will happen to the ball.

Talking about a balanced finish position and a perfect pose reminds me of a photo of one of the most amazing moments in golf history. The photo was taken during the 1950 U.S. Open at Merion Golf Club (Ardmore, PA) as Ben Hogan held his finish position and watched his 1-iron shot fly toward the green. The shot was from the middle of the 18th fairway on the final day. Mr. Hogan needed a par to force a playoff.

It was a miracle that he was even competing, as this was Mr. Hogan's first tournament back after being in a car crash that nearly killed him. Mr. Hogan's car collided head-on with a Greyhound bus. He fractured his collarbone, pelvis, and ankle, and crushed one of his ribs. The doctors told him his golf career was over. Obviously, Mr. Hogan did not accept that diagnosis and, sixteen months later, he was fighting to win the prestigious U.S. Open.

The U.S. Open always provides great physical and mental challenges for players by the manner in which the United States Golf Association (USGA) sets up the golf course. It was an even greater test in the early days, as the schedule included 36 holes of play on the final day, unlike the 18 holes played in the modern day. The physical toll of the day was almost too much for Mr. Hogan. David Barrett, author of *Miracle at Merion*,[29] shares that, on the 12th hole, Mr. Hogan almost fell down and he could barely walk after that. Mr. Hogan himself admitted that he almost quit after the 13th hole. But he would not give up, carrying on in the spirit of Vince Lombardi's saying, "Winners never quit and quitters never win."[30] Mr. Hogan's playing partner and competitor, Cary Middlecoff, actually marked Mr. Hogan's golf ball on the greens because Mr. Hogan was in agony from the searing pain in his legs caused by every step.

---

29 https://www.amazon.com/Miracle-Merion-Inspiring-Amazing-Comeback/dp/1616080825
30 http://www.brainyquote.com/quotes/quotes/v/vincelomba122285.html

Photo by Hy Peskin. *LIFE Magazine*, 1950 TIME Inc.

At the end of the round, Mr. Hogan needed a par on the very challenging 18th hole. He hit a drive to the middle of the fairway and then he hit the miracle shot: 1-iron onto the green. Lee Trevino said, "If you are caught on a golf course during a storm and are afraid of lightning, hold up a 1-iron. Not even God can hit a 1-iron."[31] Well, Ben Hogan could. He hit it perfectly in the perfectmoment. His ball landed on the green and he two-putted for par. Mr. Hogan's courage, mental toughness, and sheer determination helped him not only to survive the day but also finish tied for the lead, which forced a playoff.

The next day, he returned to Merion to win the 18-hole playoff over Lloyd Mangrum and George Fazio. This was the second of Mr. Hogan's four U.S. Open titles.

---

31 http://www.brainyquote.com/quotes/authors/l/lee_trevino.html

The "Miracle at Merion," as it is known, was such an amazing story of heart, strength, follow through, and finish that Hollywood made a movie about it called *Follow the Sun* just one year after his triumph.

Let's get to your follow-through so you can have that perfectly balanced finish like Ben Hogan.

Here's your first drill: Get a middle iron, such as a 7- or an 8-iron, and place your ball on a tee. Be sure to tee the ball low. Take your normal setup and swing, but after you swing through the ball, keep rotating your hips toward the target, allow your back leg to lift off the ground and take a step down the target line.

This drill will promote a full rotation through the ball and help you make a habit of transferring your weight forward. Make ten swings with the forward step after contact and then take your regular swing and hold your finish position. Feel as if you are posing for a picture. Smile at the shot you just hit because it's probably a good one.

If you find that you are falling away from the target in your finish, go back to the Step-Forward Drill for another ten swings. You can do it. You can make this improvement in your swing. When you go back to your regular swing, hold your finish and tap your back foot three times. This will ensure that your weight is on your lead leg.

You can also improve your follow-through and finish position even when you're indoors without a club. You only need a mirror. Get into your setup position with the mirror to your side, as if it were the target. Tilt forward, let your arms hang relaxed, and look at the spot on the floor where your golf ball would be located. Turn your shoulders back as if you're making a backswing, allowing your weight to shift onto your trail leg. Then, start to transition into your forward swing. Unwind your hips, let your arms drop, swing through impact, and continue to follow through by rotating your upper body. Allow your arms to swing toward the target (your mirror) and then to the finish, above your lead shoulder. As you look into the mirror, your goal is to see your belt buckle pointing at the target or a little past it, but your upper body should be rotated as far as your flexibility will allow. If you are as flexible as Michelle Wie and Rickie Fowler, you'll see your trail shoulder in the mirror.

Make at least ten swings in front of the mirror and hold your finish. You'll feel a stretch in your lower back. Try to rotate a little more each time. You may be thinking, "Debbie, that's not a real swing. I'm not even hitting a ball and I don't even have a golf club in my hand. How can this help?" Actually, it's easier to make an effective golf swing when you are *not* hitting a golf ball. Repeating the movements of a great swing is a key to making it automatic.

The mental strategy of the game when it comes to your follow-through is very simple. As you practice, say the word "finish" to yourself every time you swing to a complete finish. When you watch golf on television and a professional completes his or her swing, say "finish" in your mind. You are training your brain to know exactly what the word "finish" means and feels like for your full swing. Now, when you are playing, once you address the ball and take one last look at your target, say the word "finish" in your mind right before you begin your swing. It works! So often in golf, we think too much before, during, and after the swing. Use one word—*finish*—to help you follow through to a balanced finish position. Something good will happen at impact when you get to a great finish position.

Follow through with your practice, indoors and out, and your swing will improve. Hold your finish as if you were Ben Hogan posing for a picture.

Follow Through in Life

How is your follow-through in life? When you set out to accomplish a goal, do you follow through? Do you continue an act or task to its conclusion? If not, how can you succeed? Will your desired outcome make your life better? That's usually the point of achieving a goal—to make something better in your life.

Let's look at some statistics on New Year's resolutions from the Statistic Brain Research Institute. The top ten New Year's resolutions for 2015 were to lose weight, get organized, spend less, save more, enjoy life to the fullest, stay fit and healthy, learn something exciting, quit smoking, help others in their dreams, fall in love, and spend more time with family.

Forty-five percent of Americans usually make New Year's resolutions, but only 8 percent are successful in achieving their resolutions. Only 75 percent of people maintain their resolutions through the first week, and the numbers drop after that. After two weeks, 71 percent of people are maintaining their resolutions; after one month, 64 percent are still going; and after six months, only 46 percent are maintaining their resolutions.[32]

To successfully keep your New Year's resolution or reach any goal take some time to work through the Core Triumph! formula for success. Think of an area you want to make even better or a goal you would like to achieve.

Coach: What *coach or mentor* will you engage?

_____

Outcome: Be very specific about the exact *outcome* or resolution?

_____

_____

Reasons: Make your reasons as compelling and meaningful as possible. An example of a compelling reason is to be healthy and active enough to play with your children.

_____

_____

_____

_____

Execution: If your reasons are compelling and important to you, executing with energy will be easy. How will you follow through?

_____

_____

_____

_____

---

32 http://www.statisticbrain.com/new-years-resolution-statistics/

"Tri:" Take the time to analyze your progress. Is your *execution* plan working? If not, don't change the *outcome*, try something different in your *execution* plan. Talk with your *coach*.

Celebrate!: Be sure to celebrate your successes!

This is your plan for CORE Triumph!

Follow through. You can do this. Continue to review your reasons and stick to your plan. If the plan isn't getting you the outcome you desire, then adjust your plan. Don't quit. Start right now! What can you do in this very moment to get started? Do something right now. Put down this book and do something now. Make a phone call to schedule something, find a coach (the *C* in CORE Triumph!), go for a walk, throw your cigarettes away, check your bank account, or text your partner and set up a date night or just say "I love you!"

Use my acronym FAN to remind yourself to be your own number one fan. FAN stands for *Focused Action Now*! Action is a key to success!

Begin, follow through, and Triumph! The next chapter will teach you how to make a habit of achieving your goals by getting very specific with your execution plan.

Chapter 8: Key Elements

Here are the key elements covered in Chapter 8:

- The golf ball is not the target.
- Use the Step-Forward Drill to make your follow-through even better.
- Practice your swing in front of a mirror.
- Say the word "finish" when you see a professional golfer get to a balanced finish position. This programs the visual picture with the word in your mind.
- Say the word "finish" to yourself before your swing.
- Follow through and achieve your goals by making your reasons compelling enough to motivate you.
- Be your best FAN and take *Focused Action Now*!

Nine

SHORT GAME AND SHORT-TERM GOALS

A goal is a dream with a deadline.

—NAPOLEON HILL

In this chapter, we will review the fundamentals of one of the most important short-game shots: the chip-and-run. This shot is a core ingredient to lower scores. We will also discuss the power of short-term goals and their importance in reaching your dreams.

Coaches	Outcome	Reasons	Execution
• Debbie O'Connell	• Lower golf scores	• Feel awesome shooting lower golf scores	• Read this chapter
• B. F. Skinner	• Gain confidence in chipping	• Feel confident stepping up to a chip shot	• Work through this chapter
	• Begin to achieve small goals on the way to achieving a major personal goal	• Make goals more attainable	• Plan time to practice chipping using the drills in this chapter
			• Set short term goals to achieve on the way to reaching a larger goal

You hear it all the time about golf: If you want to lower your score, practice your short game. What is the short game exactly? Well, in my opinion, it is any shot less than a full swing—from putting to a three-quarter swing and everything in between.

Let's start with the chip-and-run. In Chapter 4, we talked about the benefits of practicing the chip-shot technique to improve many areas of your game. I'm going to share a few drills to make your chip shots even better.

To begin, lean about 70 percent of your weight toward the target and keep it there throughout the shot. You will actually finish with a little more than 70 percent of your weight forward. Many of my students who struggle with this shot have a tendency to shift their weight away from the target during this shot. Your brain's instinct with this short shot is to lean away from the target and lift, or scoop, the ball into the air, but the exact opposite is the most effective. Keep your weight forward and, as you start your forward swing, turn your hips toward the target and swing the club down through the grass, keeping the clubhead low to the ground as long as your arc permits.

Here's a drill to help you achieve a perfect chip shot: Once you set up, put all of your weight on your lead foot. Pick up your trail foot and rest your toes on the ground behind your lead foot, just to help you stay balanced. Make some chip-and-run shots in this stance. If you lose your balance because you are falling away from the target, this drill is perfect for you. You can even practice this way in front of your mirror without a ball. Notice how the technique looks and feels.

I also want to increase your confidence with this shot, so here is another great drill: Practice the chip-and-run shot with your eyes closed, but be sure to keep your eyes open until you get set up. I've had many students who actually hit the ball better this way. Remember, golf is not about hand-eye coordination. It's about making a consistent movement and allowing the club to swing in an arc. The ball just gets in the way at the bottom of the arc. After you hit the ball well with your eyes closed, make this statement: "This shot is so easy I can do it with my eyes closed!" You can!

Another challenge you may be experiencing with your chip shot is to stay in your tilt through impact. It's not that you are looking up. You know you don't even have to see the ball to hit it. You are standing up. To stop that habit, do this drill: Line up six golf balls parallel to the green. You are going to swing the golf club back and through without stopping. As the club is swinging back, take two steps toward the golf ball and swing through it. Don't even look to see where it goes. You won't have time as you are stepping toward the next ball. You can line up as many golf balls as you like. I've even lined up 10 to 15 golf balls to execute this drill. You will definitely stay in the tilt.

Now it's time to practice like you play. At the practice area, toss just one golf ball on the ground close to, but not on, the putting green. Pick a target you will chip to. Engage with the same focus and intensity you have while you play. Go through your pre-shot routine and make your shot. If the ball did not go into the hole, get your putter and putt until you finish the hole. This is a game-like situation that will help you prepare to successfully execute this shot on the golf course. Set a goal for yourself, such as making at least five up-and-downs (one chip and one putt) out of ten shots. Or, even better, chipping it in three times before you finish practicing. Change your goal based on your level of play. You want to make it challenging enough that you have to focus and feel a little pressure, but it shouldn't be so far out of reach that you don't come close to your goal. It will be very rewarding as you see improvement. Keep making your goals a bit more challenging as you improve.

Practicing this way is even more fun with a friend. Instead of just challenging yourself, you can have competitions with your friend.

Life's Short Term Goals

Working on your short game will help you achieve a larger goal of lowering your golf scores or handicap. You can relate this to accomplishing any long-term goal in life. Set short-term goals on your way to triumph on a larger goal. For example, if you set a goal to lose weight, the long-term goal may be ten, twenty, fifty, or more pounds. The thought of losing that much weight could be daunting. If you break it down into short-term goals, such as losing two pounds in one week, it becomes easier to achieve. Or you can break it down even more by setting a goal to avoid eating pasta and fried foods for one day. At the end of the day, you will feel successful and the accomplishment will motivate you to keep going.

Sometimes when you set your goal, you need to change a behavior to accomplish it. Psychologist B. F. Skinner introduced and tested a method used to enforce behavioral changes called "successive approximation."[33] After all, in order to reach a goal, some behavior needs to change. By setting short-term goals and giving yourself positive reinforcement when the goals are accomplished, your behavior begins to change.

---

33 About Behaviorism, BF Skinner 1974

In the example weight-loss goal above, you want to change your behavior of overeating or indulging in an unhealthy diet. To reinforce your new behavior, celebrate and reward yourself for a day without pasta or fried foods. That will make you want to succeed again. Just don't celebrate with an ice cream sundae. Choose another reward. It could be just putting your arms in the air, smiling, jumping up and down, and saying, "Yes, I did it!" Act as if you just made a hole-in-one. That will feel great. Maybe you could reward yourself by taking a bath and relaxing or by watching a favorite movie. What will make you happy? Maybe when you shed the first ten pounds, you could buy yourself something that you've always wanted. By rewarding yourself for a series of successes, you will continue to create and maintain new habits.

In his research of changing behavior, B. F. Skinner actually taught pigeons to play ping-pong. The pigeons would peck a ping-pong ball, hitting it back and forth across a small table. The table had railings on both sides to prevent the ball from falling off. If the defending pigeon failed to peck the ball back, allowing it to roll off the end of the table, a mechanism would open, revealing food for the opposing pigeon. I was amazed to read that pigeons could rally for up to six returns.

So, how did he train the pigeons? He trained one bird at a time with short-term goals:

> First, the bird was rewarded just for pecking a table tennis ball fixed to the edge of the playing table. Once the bird reliably pecked the ball in one position, the ball was moved to another place until the pigeon was willing to peck it wherever it might be found. The next stage was to train the bird to peck the ball when it was free to roll around. The final stage, before introducing each pigeon to its opponent in the game, was to reward the bird only if it succeeded in pecking the ball so that the ball hit a bar placed across the playing table. Finally, the birds were introduced to each other and rewarded for scoring points past each other. (Wynne and Udell, 2013)

B. F. Skinner used successive approximation to train dogs, pigeons, and chickens. Humans are trainable, too. The key is to look at your massive goal, break it down into a series of smaller short-term goals, and reinforce the new behavior with a reward or celebration. The more you reward yourself and celebrate achievements, the more inspired and motivated you will be to keep going.

This is really important when it comes to changing a habit or creating a new habit. As an example, let's say you want to start getting up early to exercise every weekday. The night before you are going to start, cue up your favorite song on your iPod, phone, or CD player. Set your alarm just five minutes earlier than normal. When your alarm sounds, get right up, and play your song. Dance to it, sing along, or just listen, but definitely notice how happy it makes you feel. Be sure not to hit snooze and roll over, telling yourself you'll start tomorrow. You already made the decision the night before. If getting up is a struggle, think of a few of your reasons why you want to achieve your ultimate outcome. Remember, your reasons are your motivation!

After you are comfortable with this routine, get up an additional five minutes earlier - making it ten minutes from your original start time - and start doing some exercises to your music. You'll feel great! Reinforce this new behavior by thinking awesome thoughts, such as, "Oh, yeah, I'm taking care of my body," "I'm looking better already," "I'm getting healthier and creating more energy every day," and "I love to get up early and start moving!"

Continue to add more and more minutes of exercise until you reach your goal for the length of your workout period. Soon, you'll wake up and pop out of bed, ready to start the day.

Years ago, when I was in my early twenties, I decided to start jogging every day. I was not in very good cardiovascular shape at the time. I set my alarm to get up early and I started jogging. I could only jog about two-tenths of a mile, and then I walked. The next day, I jogged a little bit farther before I started to walk. Each day, I pushed myself to jog beyond where I had gone the previous day. Some days, it was only a step or two, but other days, I was able to do significantly more. My goal was to be able to run five miles without walking at all. I had my route mapped out, so after I could jog at least one mile, I would walk the rest of the five-mile path. Every day, I succeeded in my goal to jog farther than I had the previous day and I felt triumphant. Before I knew it, I was popping out of bed with excitement and energy before the alarm sounded and jogging the full five miles.

Now I like to use workout videos for my training. I really enjoy the variety of routines in Tony Horton's P90X® fitness series. He even has a 10-minute training video series. I also do many exercises I learned from my TPI (Titleist Performance Institute) training. To build muscle, I train with Sagi Kalev's DVD series called Body Beast. If you like to dance, just search the Internet for dance workouts and you'll find many. I've also done Zumba, which is a blast.

My best trainer is my dog, Mickey. We go for a nearly two-mile walk, jog, run, sniff, pee, and poop (he does the sniffing, peeing, and pooping) almost every day. Part of my motivation is to keep Mickey healthy. He is fifteen years old. Mickey is one of my reasons in my CORE Triumph! plan for health and fitness.

Let's use CORE Triumph! to set a plan to reach one of your goals. You can use the same outcome from the previous chapter.

Coach: Write down a coach, teacher or mentor you'll engage for one of your goals.

_____

Outcome: Write down a significant goal.

_____

_____

_____

Reasons: It's very important to review and add to your reasons.

_____

_____

_____

_____

_____

Execution: Include small, easy-to-achieve goals along the way. How will you reward yourself for achieving the short term goal?

1._____

Reward _____

2._____

Reward _____

3._____

Reward _____

4._____

Reward _____

5._____

Reward _____

Chapter 9: Key Elements

Here are the key elements covered in Chapter 9:

- Practice your chip-and-run shot to lower your golf score.
- Do drills to help you to create good habits in your technique.
- Practice like you play by chipping and then putting out.
- Set short-term goals in life to achieve your dreams.
- Celebrate when you are successful in your short-term goals.

Ten

Fly Over Obstacles

There are plenty of difficult obstacles in your path.
Don't allow yourself to become one of them.

—Ralph Marston

In this chapter, you will learn the fundamentals of a pitch shot, which is a key shot to hit the ball high over obstacles in order for it to land softly on the green. We will also examine strategies to overcome obstacles or challenges that are on the path to your ideal outcome. Below, find the CORE Triumph! plan for this chapter.

Coaches	Outcome	Reasons	Execution
• Debbie O'Connell	• Execute successful pitch shots	• Lower golf scores	• Read this chapter
• Tatyana McFadden	• Have the knowledge and confidence to hit the ball over obstacles	• More fun playing golf	• Work through this chapter
• Dr. Gail Matthews	• Gain confidence and learn how to overcome challenges	• Recognize that golf and life are full of challenges	• Practice HAT for your pitch shot
		• Know you can handle anything	• Be aware of obstacles
		• Less stress in life	• Focus on what you can do to get over, around, or through obstacles
		• Get past all challenges	• Write your plan
		• Succeed and feel proud	• Be accountable to someone

Sometimes in golf and life, we have to get over obstacles or challenges. How do you handle challenging situations? Do you go around them or over them? Do you focus on the obstacle or the goal? I like what Ralph Marston said at the beginning of this chapter: There will always be obstacles on the golf course and in life; how you react and handle those obstacles are key to your success. Focus on where you are going, and find a way to get over, through, or around whatever is in your way.

In golf, it's important that you know your own game and your strengths as well as your areas that need some improvement. When you are close to the green, you'll often need to fly the ball over a greenside bunker or the rough to get onto the green. Part of the plan for success is to know your outcome. Picture the ball flying through the air and landing in the perfect place. Once you have assessed the situation and made your decisions about club selection and the flight of the ball, no longer focus on, look at, or think about the obstacle. Focus on your target.

The shot you want to use is called a pitch shot. A pitch shot is one that flies high in the air and lands softly on the green. It is not a full swing. It's great to use when you are hitting to a hole that is close to the fringe leaving you very little green between you and the hole. In that situation, you don't want the ball to roll very much when it lands on the green.

Here's your technique: I call it HAT (Hinge, Accelerate, and Target). Your backswing starts by turning with the big muscles in your upper back and shoulders (just like the chip shot), and then your hands will hinge. The length of your backswing will be determined by the distance you want the ball to travel in the air. It's best if you practice various length swings to determine how far your golf ball will travel. This is unique to each individual. I suggest you take some time to practice one-quarter, half, and three-quarter backswings, and learn how far each swing makes the ball travel. If you need about a half backswing for your shot—meaning that your lead arm is parallel to the ground when you complete the backswing—your arm and club will look like a letter *L*. From there, let your arms drop so they swing down and forward and accelerate through impact. You may be like many of my students who take the club back too far and then slow down through impact. These students struggled to hit the pitch shot successfully. You always want your clubhead to accelerate through the ball, but don't have the sensation of pushing—just keep swinging through impact.

Keep the club swinging toward your target. The mechanics are very similar to a full swing, just shorter. One difference is you want to start with about 60 percent of your weight on your forward foot so you are leaning toward the target. Keep your weight there during your backswing, but then as you start your forward swing, turn your hips toward the target and allow even more weight to shift onto that lead leg.

For different length pitch shots, you just change the length of your backswing, resulting in a longer follow-through. When more distance is required, swing the club farther back, and you will have a little more clubhead speed as the club swings through impact, resulting in a longer and higher shot. Remember HAT, *hinge* in the backswing, let the club *accelerate* to the *target*.

One of my students was struggling to get the feel of the varying lengths of his backswings. During our conversations, he mentioned that he was very good at Cornhole, which is a game where a player tosses a bean bag toward a raised platform that has holes in it. If the bean bag goes into the hole, you score three points, and if it lands on the platform, you get one point. I had him pretend that he was tossing the golf ball toward the hole, just as he does when he plays Cornhole. With this visualization, he was able to adjust the length of his backswing for different yardages and allow the clubhead to swing toward the target.

Practice tossing a golf ball underhand into a basket or to a spot on the green to improve your feel for the pitch shot. Start close to your target and slowly move away. You'll find that you will instinctively swing your arm back farther to toss the ball farther. We all have an innate ability to judge distance. I'm going to make a brave assumption here: Most of the time, you stop your car before you hit the car in front of you at a red light or stop sign, correct? I bet you always leave a similar amount of space between your car and the next as well. You see, you have a sense of distance. Trust that instinct on the golf course.

To pitch the ball into the air, remember HAT (Hinge, Accelerate, and Target). Hinge and let the club accelerate to the target. Practice this technique at the practice area or in your yard to get comfortable with feeling your hinge. Seeing yourself in a mirror will help, as well. Be sure to feel the clubhead drop, accelerate, and then swing toward your target. You'll be amazed at just how easy this shot is when you use HAT. Hats off to you for a terrific pitch shot that will get you over obstacles.

Hinge

Accelerate to the target

Getting Over Life's Obstacles

Getting over or through obstacles in life requires focusing on the target and what's possible with a positive attitude. I once had the opportunity to meet an extraordinary person who has had to overcome tremendous obstacles from birth. Tatyana McFadden was born with a disease called spina bifida, which is a hole in the spine. Tatyana is paralyzed from the waist down. She spent the first six-and-a-half years of her life in an orphanage in Russia, without access to a wheelchair. Tatyana had some big obstacles. She did not see it that way. She wanted to keep up with the other children and play, so she figured out a way. Tatyana learned to walk on her hands. She did not accept a limiting belief that she could not play because she could not walk. When there is a will, there is a way, and Tatyana found a way.

Tatyana was adopted in 1994 by an American woman, Deborah McFadden, who was then the commissioner of disabilities for what is now the U.S. Department of Health and Human Services. Although Tatyana had an exciting new life and more opportunities, her health got worse. Her family was even told that she might only live a couple more years. To gain strength with the hopes of improving her health, Deborah enrolled Tatyana in various sports programs, including wheelchair basketball, swimming, ice hockey, and scuba diving. She found her passion—wheelchair racing. Her health improved drastically, and she became an incredibly strong world-class athlete. Tatyana always rose higher than any challenge that life presented her.

She made her debut in the 2004 Paralympics when she was just fifteen years old; she was the youngest person on the US Team. Tatyana won two medals in 2004. In 2008, she brought home four medals. In 2012, she added another four medals to her collection, three of which were gold. At the 2013 World Championships, she became the first athlete in history to win six gold medals at the same competition. Tatyana brought home four more gold and two silver medals from the Rio 2016 Paralympics.

Always up for a challenge, Tatyana joined the professional marathon circuit. She has won the Boston, Chicago, London, and New York marathons.

She is the first person, able bodied or disabled, to win the grand slam—four major world marathons in the same year. In 2016 she completed her fourth straight Grand Slam! She also competes in the winter Paralympics in cross-country skiing, winning a silver medal in 2014.

Tatyana's drive is inspiring. Her vision of the world is always about what is possible. I love the quote that reads, "Nothing is impossible…the word itself says, 'I'm possible!'" Tatyana McFadden understands the challenge in front of her and then finds a way to rise above it.[34]

Sometimes your obstacle is bumper-to-bumper traffic and the only way to get to your destination is to go through it. Instead of thinking about the traffic and getting frustrated, focus on what you can do with that time. Whom can you call? What appointment can you make? Can you record some notes about a project or a goal you're working on? Think about your best golf game and all of the awesome shots you have played. Make the most of your time. After all, time is precious. Use it wisely.

One time when I was in traffic, I started thinking about my Christmas gift list. It was most likely December 20th. I grabbed my phone and recorded a list of names and gift ideas for each person. It made my last-minute shopping much easier. I know you probably finish your shopping well before I start mine. The point is to do something constructive with the time when you are in traffic, waiting for a delayed flight, sitting on a runway, or standing in a long line. Focus on what you can do and what you can control—you'll enjoy the experience much more and feel proud of yourself for accomplishing something. That's so much better than getting angry and indulging in self-pity because you were stuck. It's your choice whether to be stuck and miserable, or to be inspired and accomplish something.

---

34 http://tatyanamcfadden.com

Fly Over Life's Obstacles

How do successful people reach their goals despite challenges? Let's face it: The road to achievement is not always smooth. There may be a bunker or a water hazard in the way. Sometimes, the obstacle is our own limiting beliefs that tell us we're not good enough or we'll never succeed. Let's get you over, through, or around any challenge that could derail you on your way to achieving your ideal outcome.

Dr. Gail Matthews, a psychology professor at Dominican University of California, performed a study on how goal achievement in the workplace is influenced by writing goals, making action plans, and being accountable to others. Participants were randomly assigned to one of five groups. Here is a summary of the groups:

- Group 1 thought about their goals.
- Group 2 wrote down their goals.
- Group 3 wrote down their goals and action commitments for each goal.
- Group 4 did the same as Group 3 and then shared that work with a friend.
- Group 5 did the same as Group 4 and sent weekly progress reports.

After four weeks, just 43 percent of Group 1 had accomplished their goals or were at least halfway there, while 76 percent of Group 5 had either accomplished their goals or were at least halfway there.

Dr. Matthews concluded, "My study provides empirical evidence for the effectiveness of three coaching tools: accountability, commitment, and writing down one's goals."[35]

I have many coaches and I appreciate and need all of them. In writing this book, I leaned heavily on Coach Lisa from the Anthony Robbins Research Company. After I had completed seven chapters of this book, everything slowed down. I couldn't seem to get myself focused on writing.

---

35 http://www.dominican.edu/dominicannews/study-highlights-strategies-for-achieving-goals

Actually, I couldn't even get started. Each time I sat at my computer, I would check e-mails, remember I needed to order something from Amazon, and click on some other links for shopping, or I would notice a drawer was disorganized when I was looking for something and start cleaning the drawer. It seemed as if almost everything was more important than working on my book.

I was very aware of my behavior and I felt frustrated with myself. I was thinking, "I understand all of this, so why am I procrastinating?" Procrastination was an old behavior and limiting belief that I had. I was embarrassed to tell my coach that I was struggling because for so long I had been a rock star. I needed her to help me through this rough patch. One of her strategies was to make me accountable. We made a schedule for Chapters 9–12. Each chapter had a deadline for completion. We also broke down each chapter and listed the steps it would take to complete the chapter and made a deadline for each step. The first step for each chapter was to go through and write down my CORE Triumph! plan, which included deadlines for completing the research, rough draft, and final copy. She had me e-mail her every week with a progress report—accountability. Coach Lisa also encouraged me to ask my family for support, encouragement, and accountability. I surrounded myself with people who knew my desired outcome and the challenge I was experiencing. I asked for their help.

If you are reading this book, it worked! There is no shame in asking for help. After all, we are only human. That does not mean you are weak or uninspired or unmotivated. It means that you are self-aware and brilliant. Many people get excited about a new idea, goal, or project, and bolt out of the gate, creating a thunderous roar like twenty thoroughbreds starting the Kentucky Derby. The challenge is the race to your goal, which usually takes longer than the "most exciting two minutes in sports," as the Kentucky Derby is often described. Your race is more like a marathon. There are times when you feel tired and alone, when you have doubts and maybe even fall down. That's why it's important to have people cheering for you and making you accountable throughout the entire race until you cross the finish line. I ran (well, jogged and walked) a half marathon years ago, but I still remember the inspiration and energy I felt as spectators cheered me on. So don't be afraid to ask your circle of family and friends to be part of your journey. Often the journey itself is the best part of striving for a desired outcome. Enjoy the team effort that it sometimes requires.

If you are like me, you love a movie that shows the challenges, the incredible dedication, and the effort against all odds on the way to the victory. I cry at the triumph. The more difficulties, challenges, and rejections there are, the more I cry because of the true grit, focus, and plain hard work that were needed to succeed. Some of my favorite movies include *Secretariat, Remember the Titans, The Pursuit of Happyness, Rudy,* and *Iron Jawed Angels.*

CORE Triumph! works. Having a Coach makes you accountable. Writing down your Outcome works because you will see your goals. Writing down your Reasons for wanting to reach your outcome seals your commitment. Executing your plan—once you have defined your big goals—works by setting short-term goals to achieve your desired outcome.

List any challenges you want to overcome.

_____

_____

_____

_____

Coach: Write down who can *coach,* encourage, and hold you accountable.

_____

_____

_____

_____

Outcome: What is your clear *outcome?*

_____

_____

Reasons: What are the compelling *reasons* for this outcome?

_____

_____

_____

Execution: Create your *execution* plan and add deadlines for certain tasks on your way to your *outcome*. Plan the accomplishment celebration (we will examine the importance of celebrating more in the next chapter).

_____

_____

_____

_____

_____

Chapter 10: Key Elements

Here are the key elements covered in Chapter 10:

- Focus on your outcome when an obstacle arises.
- Use HAT for your pitch shot (Hinge, Accelerate, and Target).
- Be sure your thoughts and discussions are on positive things and the outcome you desire.
- Be open with your coach or mentor if you are struggling.

Eleven

ACHIEVE AND CELEBRATE

The more you praise and celebrate your life,
the more there is in life to celebrate.

—OPRAH WINFREY

My goal has always been not to look to the next thing, but
to relish and celebrate the successes I have at the moment,
whether it's landing a part in a student film or having a
good day in acting class. I never discredit anything.

—DIANNA AGRON

Coaches	Outcome	Reasons	Execution
• Debbie O'Connell	• Be an even better putter	• Play better golf	• Read this chapter
• Teresa Amabile	• Lower golf scores	• Live a happier life	• Work through this chapter
• Steven J. Kramer	• Celebrate every day, throughout the day	• Create more success	• Pay attention to all of the good things that happen during a round of golf and a day of life
• Shelly L. Gable		• Feel triumphant	
• Gian C. Gonzaga		• Be more creative and perform better in all aspects of life	• Celebrate all successes
• Amy Strachman			• Plan celebrations
			• Practice patting yourself on the back
			• Congratulate yourself and smile

We all experience many triumphs during a round of golf and throughout every day of life. I think we should all celebrate more. When you make a putt on the hole, say, "Yes, way to go!" Be your own cheerleader and best friend. If you had a more challenging journey from the tee box to the green, reward yourself for hanging in there and finishing the hole. If your playing partner was struggling, I don't believe you would say, "Wow! That was awful. You really messed up on that hole!" So why do we feel the need to criticize ourselves so severely?

Do you ask yourself, "What's wrong with me?" Remember—in the first chapter, we met Joe Matson, who taught us about asking quality questions to gain a desired outcome. Well, if you are asking negative questions, your brain and the universe will focus on and find those answers, as well. Questions, such as, "Why can't I get better at this game?" "Why do I always make an eight on this hole?" or "How could I be so stupid or lazy?" are not empowering questions helping you reach your goals.

What about asking questions like these: "What can I learn from that hole, shot, or situation?" "How can I do better?" or "What did I do right?" Getting your brain to work on positive solutions and answers will make you feel better. Your thoughts will determine how you feel, so make your thoughts and questions empowering.

Early on in my golfing career, I played a round of golf with my mom and a couple of friends. I did not play well and my self-criticism was awful. I was so hard on myself because I was always a talented athlete who had accomplished much in sports, but I was struggling with this game of golf. Beating myself up did not make me play better. It did the opposite. I would hit a bad shot and think, "See? I can't play this game!" I'm sure I was not any fun to be around that day.

After the round, I thought about the day and realized that I was being ridiculous. I apologized to my playing partners and then to myself. I looked myself in the eyes and said aloud, "I am so sorry for the way I treated you today. I will never do that to you again!" I never have.

That's not to say I never get frustrated at a poor shot. I do sometimes, but only for a brief moment. I don't call myself stupid or a bad golfer. I will recognize that it was a poor decision or a bad shot and then say something positive or ask a quality question.

I have an assignment for you. Play your next round of golf or go through a day in life without criticizing yourself. The first step to this assignment is to be aware of your thoughts. You may be so used to having negative thoughts about yourself that you don't even realize it. So, first, pay attention. If you notice yourself thinking or saying something critical, think "stop" or "cancel," and instead say something else: "I can do better," "I'll learn from that experience," "Great effort," or "I'm proud of you!"

The second part of the assignment is to celebrate. This is the exclamation in CORE Triumph! Throughout the day, make a fist pump and say "yes" when something goes well. Think, "Way to go!" and give yourself a pat on the back with every accomplishment. You will have a blast and you will feel happy and accomplished all day long.

For one of your larger goals, plan a significant reward and celebration for when you reach that ideal outcome. It is so important to celebrate. Life is meant to be celebrated.

When you play golf, you have nine or eighteen opportunities to celebrate achieving your goal of completing the hole. Hopefully, you will also celebrate at the 19th hole (the gathering place at the club called a lounge, restaurant or bar) after your round. Celebrate all of the awesome shots you hit during the round. Too often, the conversations in the clubhouse are about all of the poor shots or holes that were played. Try telling a story about an awesome shot.

My hope is that you have more to celebrate on the golf course and that you are completing each hole in fewer strokes. You most likely have heard the saying by Bobby Locke, "Drive for show. Putt for dough!"[36] Locke, a PGA professional, was outstanding and often scored well in tournaments because of his extraordinary putting. He collected a lot of dough in his seventy-four professional wins.

Now, let's examine a critical stroke in the game—one that ends every hole, except for those times you may hit the ball in from off the green. We will make your putting even better so you can roll the ball into the hole and celebrate. LPGA Tour professional Christina Kim shows very animated celebrations on the golf course. She exhibits a great amount of emotion and energy as she celebrates by making double fist pumps then putting her arms in the air. Come up with your own move.

Putting technique is as easy as one, two, three, and four. Three parts of your body stay still during your putting stroke: your head, your wrists, and your lower body. The fourth part of the formula refers to the setup—when

---

36 http://www.brainyquote.com/quotes/quotes/b/bobbylocke115444.html

you get your eyes directly over the ball or within two inches of it. You don't want your eyes to be on the other side of the ball.

With your eyes above the ball and your head, wrists, and lower body still, you will make an awesome putting stroke. Since you don't always feel what is real in any golf swing, I'd like you to make some putts in front of a mirror. Instead of looking down at the golf ball, watch yourself in the mirror.

First, watch your head. On the next stroke, watch your wrists; and on the third stroke, focus on your lower body. If you find that you are moving any of those body parts, you'll want to spend some time improving that area of your stroke.

Here are some drills that will help:

- The first drill is one you can practice at home to keep your head still. You'll need your putter, a few golf balls, a pillow, and a wall. Stand close to the wall, facing it, while holding your pillow. Get into your setup, place the pillow against the wall and hold it there with your head. Make your putting stroke while keeping your head still. You may feel silly doing this, but it will be worth your time because it works.
- If your wrists are moving during your putting stroke, use the Professional Anti–Scoopy Poopie grip that we used for chipping in Chapter 4. Place your lead hand at the bottom of the grip and let the grip rest against your forearm. Hold the grip and your forearm together with your trail hand. PGA Tour Champions professional Bernhard Langer used to putt with this grip. As you make your stroke, feel your upper back and shoulders moving, allowing your putter to swing back and through like a pendulum.
- To keep your lower body still, set up with your backside against the wall and practice many putts.

Drills are important because it's challenging to just think about the proper technique and then create it. We don't always feel what is truly happening with our bodies. Once you practice with a drill guaranteeing a proper technique, you will be able to repeat it. With a solid repeatable technique, you'll be able to develop great feel for the speed of the putting greens, which is how fast the ball will roll.

The two main keys to great putting are proper pace and starting the golf ball on your intended line. It's important to learn the speed of the putting greens before your round of golf. I suggest you take three golf balls to the green and pick a hole to putt toward. Take five normal walking steps away from the hole and putt your three golf balls. Your goal is to roll the ball at a pace that leaves the ball either in the hole or just past the hole. Walk ten steps from the hole and putt, then fifteen steps and, finally, twenty steps from the hole. This will give you a great feel for the pace of the greens. As you are playing, you can count your steps from the hole to your ball to give you more information about the necessary pace you'll need to make the putt or leave it close.

Putt positively by making a practice stroke looking at the hole, feeling the perfect pace, and visualizing the ball going into the hole. You'll have a great deal of confidence when you set up and make your putt.

Having a feel for the speed of the putting green is one part of the formula for success; proper alignment is the other part of the formula. There are a couple of strategies to assist with your alignment. Some golfers will find a spot on the green a few inches in front of their golf ball where they would like the ball to roll over. When they place their putter behind the golf ball, they will aim the putter at that spot. It's much easier to aim the putter at a spot a few inches in front of the ball than it is to aim at a point farther away.

Another strategy to help start your golf ball rolling on your intended line is to use a line on your golf ball like an arrow that is pointing toward your target. Some golf ball companies are printing a line with an arrow on their golf balls or you can make a line on your golf ball with a permanent marker. Stand behind the ball - in line with your target - when you are placing your ball onto the putting green. Carefully aim the line on your ball toward your intended target. After your pre-shot routine, set the lines on your putter up as a linear pairing, meaning the line on your ball and the line on your putter should look like one line. If your putter has two parallel lines, be sure the line on your golf ball is parallel to the lines on the putter. At this point, be confident you are lined up correctly and make a confident stroke.

Here is a drill that will help you develop or reinforce a putting stroke that keeps to a steady path back and through: Practice your stroke between two golf clubs laid out parallel to each other. Use this drill for putts about five feet or closer to the hole. Set up the two golf clubs parallel to each other, with enough room for your putter to fit in between the clubs. Stroke the ball into the hole, keeping your putter between the clubs for the entire stroke.

Another way to practice getting your ball on the intended line is to make a chalk line from the hole to about five feet away. Put your ball on the line about three feet from the hole. Make your stroke, keeping the middle of your putter over the chalk line throughout your stroke.

Putt positively by always telling yourself that you are a great putter. Making a putt is a moment to celebrate. Have you ever watched a toddler or a preschool child play miniature golf? No matter how many times the child hits the ball, when the ball falls into the hole, you see pure joy and excitement on the child's face and in his or her body language. It's a celebration!

Celebrate Everyday

Many studies have been conducted about the power of celebrating success. I liked the study I read about in *Harvard Business Review* (May 2011) titled,

"The Power of Small Wins," by Teresa Amabile and Steven J. Kramer. Here is their fascinating takeaway point:

> When we think about progress, we often imagine how good it feels to achieve a long-term goal or experience a major breakthrough. These big wins are great—but they are relatively rare. The good news is that even small wins can boost inner work life tremendously. Many of the progress reports our research participants shared represented only minor steps forward. Yet they often evoked outsized positive reactions. Consider this diary entry from a programmer in a high-tech company, which was accompanied by very positive self-ratings of her emotions, motivations, and perceptions that day: "I figured out why something was not working correctly. I felt relieved and happy because this was a minor milestone for me."[37]

This study examined twelve thousand journal entries of employees from a variety of vocations, and the results showed that employees who were making progress—even small wins—are happier, more effective, and more creative workers and team members.

The study also revealed that their findings are consistent with an article published in the 1968 issue of the *Harvard Business Review* by Frederick Herzberg, titled, "One More Time: How Do You Motivate Employees?" His message about his research on the sources of employees' motivations is that, "people are most satisfied with their jobs (and therefore most motivated) when those jobs give them the opportunity to experience achievement."[38]

When I was working at a private country club, we hosted many events that required organization, cooperation, and an all-in effort by every department. The events where members could bring guests were among the most pressure packed. We wanted our members to be proud to bring their guests to their country club and we wanted to give them a first-class experience. Every department was important, but the most lasting impression came from the food

---

37 https://hbr.org/2011/05/the-power-of-small-wins
38 http://www.uvm.edu/~pdodds/files/papers/others/1968/herzberg1968.pdf

and beverage staff. I have to share that our chef and his team always stepped up. After each event, I would walk into the kitchen with a huge smile on my face, clapping my hands and loudly proclaiming, "Chef, you did it again!" I'd look around at his team and thank them for an awesome job. We would share a moment of celebration that was fun and motivational for the next occasion.

This celebratory philosophy doesn't just make an impact at the office. It will also make your romantic relationship even better.

In a study published in 2006 in the *Journal of Personality and Social Psychology*, researchers, Shelley L. Gable, Gian C. Gonzaga, and Amy Strachman, found that the way couples react to each other's good news—with excitement, pride, or indifference—is crucial in forming a strong bond. Here's an excerpt from this positive research:

> Close relationship partners often share successes and triumphs with one another, but this experience is rarely the focus of empirical study. In this study, 79 dating couples completed measures of relationship well-being and then participated in videotaped interactions in which they took turns discussing recent positive and negative events. Disclosers rated how understood, validated, and cared for they felt in each discussion, and outside observers coded responders' behavior. Both self-report data and observational codes showed that, two months later, responses to positive event discussions were more closely related to relationship well-being and break-up than were responses to negative event discussions. The results are discussed in terms of the recurrent, but often overlooked, role that positive emotional exchanges play in building relationship resources.[39]

Continue to build a strong relationship by making sure you get very excited and celebrate when your spouse, partner, boyfriend, or girlfriend shares good news with you. On that note, get overjoyed for all of your family and friends who reveal a successful event.

---

39 http://coachingtowardhappiness.com/pdf/WillYouBeThereForMeWhenThingsGoRight.pdf

Studies have proven that you will live a much happier and more successful life by being excited about and celebrating small achievements, as well as huge triumphs, whether in your relationships, work, or play on a golf course. So, pop the cork and celebrate. You are amazing and life can be one big party!

The exclamation point in CORE Triumph! is there to remind you to celebrate. Take some time to go through the exercise below to monitor your celebrations!

Write down all of the small and large successes you experienced in the last week.

_____

_____

_____

_____

_____

How do you like to celebrate (big and small)?

_____

_____

_____

_____

_____

What celebrations have you experienced in the last week?

_____

_____

_____

_____

What is the date of accomplishment for your next planned outcome or goal? How will you celebrate? Make plans now for the celebration.

_____

_____

Chapter 11: Key Elements

Here are the key elements covered in Chapter 11:

- Practice drills to make your stroke consistent.
- Improve your putting by setting up with your eyes over the ball and keeping your head, wrists, and lower body still.
- Count the number of steps from your golf ball to the hole to help with judging the pace of your putt.
- Use a strategy to correctly line up to your intended target.
- Pay attention your self-talk; make it positive and empowering.
- Celebrate everything positive, both big and small.

Twelve

Opportunities in Challenges

A pessimist sees the difficulty in every opportunity; an
optimist sees the opportunity in every difficulty.

—Winston S. Churchill

In this chapter, your CORE Triumph! plan will focus on what I like to call
opportunity shots. These are the challenging shots that offer an opportunity
to make an amazing score, despite the difficulty. These shots give you an opportunity to impress your playing partners. Like Winston Churchill said, the
optimist will see the opportunities in every challenge, both on and off the golf
course.

Coaches	Outcome	Reasons	Execution
• Debbie O'Connell	• Gain knowledge and confidence to handle opportunity shots	• Have more fun on the golf course and in life	• Read this chapter
• Bethany Hamilton	• Move past life's challenges	• Lower your golf scores	• Work through this chapter
	• Make a plan for the life you want	• Gain confidence to get through challenges	• Review and practice opportunity-shot techniques
		• Live life to the fullest	• Start each day with a thank-you list
			• Make your thoughts and words positive and forward looking

Often in golf, as in life, you find yourself in challenging situations. In order to get through those situations and move on successfully, you need to have a plan of execution, a strategy. The challenges I'm referring to include, but aren't limited to, fairway bunkers, deep rough, uphill shots, downhill shots, and shots with the ball above or below your feet. The more confident you feel when your ball settles outside the fairway, the better shot you'll hit. The more you know, understand, and hopefully practice these lies, the more confident you'll be. I call these situations *opportunity shots*. You have the opportunity to feel awesome about completing the hole successfully despite the challenges along the way.

While playing with a group of friends many years ago, I sliced my tee shot into the trees on the right side of the hole. My immediate response was a negative sigh and disappointment. I only said, "Ugh," but I definitely showed a negative response.

One of my playing partners said, "You can still make a par from there!" My attitude changed in a moment because of the possibility and the opportunity to make an awesome par after a not-so-favorable start to the hole.

When I assessed the situation, I noticed that I had an opening to hit the ball out of the woods and, with a fade, I could catch the left side of the green. I hit a pretty good shot and it faded a little but not enough to get on the green. It landed in the greenside bunker. My immediate thought this time was, "I can make par from there!"

With a confident attitude, I hit the ball out of the bunker to about five feet from the hole and proceeded to make the putt for par. You get what you focus on. My focus changed from thinking about my slice and whatever negative thoughts and questions may have followed to, "I can still make a par!"

Here are examples of some memorable opportunity shots in golf:

- **Bubba Watson's shot out of the trees at the 2012 Masters.** After a wayward drive on the downhill 10th found the trees to the right of the fairway, Bubba unleashed a huge hook with his gap wedge that landed, spun, and settled 10 feet from the hole. Here's how Bubba described it: "I hit my 52-degree, my gap wedge, hooked it about 40 yards, hit it about 15 feet off the ground until it got under the tree, and then it started rising—pretty easy." Bubba went onto victory.

- **Jordan Spieth out of a bunker at the 2013 John Deere Classic.** Jordan stepped on the par-4, 18th hole needing a birdie to get into a playoff with David Hearn and Zach Johnson. He hit his approach shot into the greenside bunker, 44 feet from the hole. Jordan stayed focused and holed out from the bunker. He went on to earn his first PGA Tour victory, becoming the youngest winner of a PGA Tour event in eighty-two years.

The part to remember about those two amazing shots is that both Bubba and Jordan hit the ball poorly in the shot just before their showstoppers. They didn't fret over their previous shots. Both Bubba and Jordan focused all of their energy on the shot they were about to hit, resulting in a successful opportunity shot. A poor beginning does not always mean a bad outcome.

Opportunity Shot: Fairway Bunker

Let's examine the techniques of some opportunity shots you may experience during your round of golf. Let's start with the fairway bunker shot. First, be sure not to call the bunker a trap. You don't want your mind to believe that you are trapped in the sand. Next, analyze the situation by looking at your lie, the position of the ball in the bunker, and the height of the lip. With this information, you'll be able to choose a club that has enough loft to get the ball over any lip. If you are deciding between two clubs, choose the club with the most loft. It's more important to get the ball out of the bunker and closer to the green than it is to risk leaving it in the bunker.

One year when I was playing in the LPGA T&CP National Championship, I hit my second shot on a par-5 into a fairway bunker that was strategically placed in the middle of the fairway. I thought I had cleared it, so I was looking 30 yards beyond the bunker and was shocked when one of my playing partners called out to tell me that my ball was in the bunker. Disappointed, I went back to my ball to look at the situation. I thought, "OK, I've got this. I can still make a great score on the hole!" I put more emphasis on reaching the green than I did in getting the ball over the lip. Well, you guessed it, I hit the top of the lip, and the ball came right back to me. It was another great learning experience in my golf history.

If there is not a significant lip to manage, look at the yardage you want the ball to go and then take one club longer than you would normally hit for the shot. This shot is as easy as **one, two, three**: Choke down about **one** inch on the grip, and play the ball about **two** inches back from its normal position with the club you will hit. This will set you up to hit the ball only at impact. Dig your feet in just a little for balance. Make a **three**-quarter backswing, and keep your lower body very still. Feel as if you are swinging with mostly your upper body and arms. Hold your finish.

Opportunity Shot: Out of the Rough

The opportunity shot of hitting the ball out of the rough has a couple of variables to consider. Analyze the depth of the rough and how deep your ball is sitting down in the long, thick grass. When hitting from the rough, try to predict how much grass you'll trap between the clubface and the ball at impact. If you catch some grass, the ball will not make direct contact with the grooves on your club and, therefore, will have less backspin. It will travel farther and roll more when it lands. When you watch golf on television, you'll hear the commentators explain when the location of the professionals golf ball is in a flyer lie, which is a shot that travels farther than intended.

If you catch a lot of grass, you'll lose swing speed and distance. Be sure to consider the grass and choose your club accordingly.

With deep rough, you want to use a more lofted club, sometimes even a pitching wedge, even if your target is not reachable with that club. The priority is to get the ball out of the rough and back onto the fairway. If your ball isn't sitting down too far, meaning you can get a club on the ball with very little grass in the way, you can use a hybrid. If you are my mother, use your 3-wood. My mom can hit her 3-wood successfully from almost anywhere. She just makes a steeper swing, digs into the rough, swings through, and watches that ball fly. It's amazing to watch.

Once you choose your club, here's your technique for hitting from the rough: Play the ball about one inch back in your stance. Lean toward the target, putting a little more weight on your lead foot. Hold on tighter with the last three fingers of your lead hand. Open up your clubface a little because the grass will close it as your club swings through the thick grass. In your swing, take the club outside your normal swing path on your initial move and swing it up by hinging early, resulting in a steeper path on the downswing. This path will allow the club to get down to the ball and hit the least amount of grass before striking the ball. Be sure to swing through toward the target. Keep your club moving forward to the finish.

During this shot, once you review your strategy, focus your mind on the target and swing your club through the grass to that target. If your focus stays on the grass and the ball, you will stop or slow down through impact instead of following through.

Opportunity Shot: Uphill Lie

There is also a technique for the opportunity shot of an uphill lie. So much about this shot is common sense, so instead of memorizing the technique,

Set up your shoulders parallel to the hill

let's make sure you understand why you make certain adjustments. Get your shoulders parallel to the slope of the hill because if your shoulders are too level, the clubhead will slam into the turf. You'll also want to swing along the slope. Because of this set up and swing, play the ball slightly more forward in your stance than normal for the club you choose to hit.

When you choose a club, take a longer club because the upward slope of the hill and the angle of your body will create more loft on your club at impact.

After you choose your target, consider that your clubface will close, so align yourself to the appropriate side. For me, as a right-handed golfer, I aim to the right of my intended target. The reason for this alignment adjustment is that, as you swing, your hands and arms will release upward through impact and cause the clubface to rotate to a closed position.

To summarize, set up to the angle of the hill and play the ball a little forward in your stance. You will hit the ball higher and shorter, and you will pull it, so pick the appropriate club and target.

Opportunity Shot: Downhill Lie

Just as you adjusted with the uphill lie, set up with your shoulders at the same angle as the slope, and swing along the slope on a downhill lie. This time, you will play the ball a little back in your stance because the ground is higher near your back foot and the club will bottom out sooner.

For your club, take a more lofted club than you would normally take for the distance because the hill will deloft the clubface, resulting in a longer shot than you would normally hit with this club.

Take a three-quarter swing with a very stable lower body. As you swing down the hill, you will have a tendency to keep the club-face open, so be sure to adjust your alignment appropriately. Set up by aiming to the pull side of your target.

Set up your shoulders parallel to the hill

To summarize, set up to the angle of the hill, and play the ball a little back in your stance.

You will hit the ball lower and longer, and you will push it, so pick the appropriate club and target.

Opportunity Shot: Sidehill Lie with Ball Above Feet

I used to struggle with the opportunity shot of having the ball above my feet, but once I started to set my weight a little more toward my toes, I began to make solid contact and swing with confidence. What I hadn't considered before was that gravity pulled me back as I made my swing, which caused me to hit the ball off the toe of the club. I made this mistake at the LPGA T&CP National Championship. The ball was above my feet, so I planned the swing properly and aimed to the right, expecting to pull the ball. Instead, as I made my swing, gravity pulled my weight to my heels and I hit the ball off the toe of my club. The ball went directly right and out of bounds. Yikes! I often tell myself that I'm an awesome teacher because I've had so many learning experiences on the golf course.

Of course, I had to hit the same shot again since it went out of bounds. This time, I set up with my weight more on my toes, made a three-quarter swing, and watched the ball go where I planned originally. Same girl, just a little more experience.

Here are the other key components to hitting a successful shot with the ball above your feet: Stand a little taller and choke down on your club since the ball is closer to you on the high side of the hill. Set your weight more toward your toes. Aim more to the push side of your target. Swing around your body—like a baseball swing with a flatter swing path. Make a three-quarter swing with a stable lower body.

Opportunity Shot: Sidehill Lie with Ball Below Feet

When the ball is below your feet, be sure to bend your knees and keep them flexed through impact. In contrast, when the ball is above your feet, get more of your weight on your heels by using the tush push.

Again, you will only use a three-quarter swing with very little lower-body movement. Stay as balanced as possible to hit a successful shot. You'll want to aim to the pull side of your target because, with the ball below your feet, it will fly toward the push side.

Balance is key for all of the opportunity shots mentioned, so only take a three-quarter swing. Take a few practice swings (except in the fairway bunker where you'll take them before you enter the bunker because the USGA Rules do not allow you to touch the ground in a hazard). Once you are 100 percent committed to how you will execute the shot, step into your proper set up, look at your target, take a deep breath, and swing. Do not be fearful of the outcome. Plan perfectly and then accept the result of your shot. Take these opportunity shots as challenges and have fun with them. Say something to yourself, such as, "I've got this!"

So, we've just reviewed how to make the most of opportunity shots on the golf course. Now, let's take a look at how those golf lessons could translate into success in other parts of your life.

Opportunity Shots in Life

How do you handle obstacles in life? Do you say you have a problem or a challenge? After reading Chapter 10, I'm sure you call them challenges. Well, let's take it a step further and call them opportunities.

The language you use can determine your effectiveness in tackling the situation. The word "problem" has a negative connotation that can elicit negative energy and fearful emotions. On the other hand, the word "challenge" sends a message that energizes and motivates you to step up and find a way to handle it. That means you can resolve the situation and make it a positive one. The word "opportunity" really gets the adrenaline going. The word alone puts you in a state of mind to tackle the situation and see the positive outcomes that will occur.

You may be going through a rough patch in life—poor health, the loss of a close relative or friend, financial struggles, addiction, relationship challenges, or a breakup. You may feel trapped or as if you are facing an uphill battle. Now ask yourself a quality question: What opportunities can you see arising from your situation? Here is your strategy for making your life better, happier, more fulfilling, and yes—in a word—awesome.

First, recognize if you are holding on to things you cannot control or that happened in the past. If something was in the past, consider it a fairway bunker hazard, pick up the rake, and smooth out your footprints. Leave that hazard the best you can by stepping out and moving on. You don't want to stay trapped by holding on too tightly to an event from your past. Holding on will lead to resentment, bitterness, and self-pity, and you may even begin to blame others for your challenges.

Release what you cannot change, especially if it was a difficult and painful experience. Of course, if you need to mourn, do it. Mourning is necessary for a short time, but not for a lifetime. Maybe you did everything right, but the situation—the job or the relationship, for example—didn't work out. If you stay in the hazard, you won't see everything awesome that life to has offer.

An outstanding example of turning a tragedy into an opportunity is the story of Bethany Hamilton, a surfer from Hawaii. A natural surfer, she began competing professionally as a young girl. However, at thirteen years old, she was attacked by a shark. She was on her surfboard when the shark bit off her left arm. Bethany nearly lost her life.

Determined not only to live but also to surf again, Bethany was back on her surfboard one month later. Her determination, positive attitude, and winning spirit led her back to competing. She didn't spend her time in self-pity, trying to figure out why the shark took her arm. Two years later, she won first place in the Explorer Women's Division of the National Scholastic Surfing Association (NSSA) National Championships. Now, as a professional surfer, she shares her inspirational message of hope with millions of people. Her story was made into an inspiring movie called *Soul Surfer*, which opened in US theaters in April 2011.[40]

Be determined like Bethany to turn adversity into opportunity. Sometimes, the opportunity is to inspire others with your strength and resilience. To live your best life, get back on the fairway, and walk forward. I once heard Joel Osteen say that if there is a period at the end of an event, don't change it into a question mark. Continuing to wonder why when there is no answer keeps you stuck. If there is something that you regret, forgive yourself. You are only human.

Move forward by paying attention to your own thoughts. Your thoughts will determine how you feel. Set yourself up each and every day with thoughts of what you are thankful for in life. Have an attitude of gratitude every morning.

---

40 http://www.beliefnet.com/entertainment/sports/galleries/5-inspiring-athletes-who-overcame-disabilities.aspx

I start each day by asking myself what I am thankful for. I always start with my family and friends, and then I just keep going. Sometimes the list includes my mattress, pillow, chairs, and cars, as well as plumbing and roads. You can find many things in life to be happy about.

When my cousin was in a motorcycle accident and broke his back, he was paralyzed from the chest down. His grandmother shared with me that when she was talking with him, she was so upset that she couldn't control her emotions. He said to her, "Grandma, I'm alive!" He did not look at what he had lost. He focused on all that he still had in life. He's an amazing young man who lives by the saying, "Crushing all limitations!"

Set yourself up for an amazing life.

Make a list of all that you have in life and the things you are thankful for.

_____

_____

_____

_____

_____

_____

What are the opportunities in your life?

_____

_____

_____

_____

Do CORE Triumph! for the life you want to see and experience.

Coaches: Who are the coaches who can help you learn to live the life you want?

_____

_____

Outcome: What is the life you imagine?

_____

_____

_____

_____

Reasons: Why do you want that life?

_____

_____

_____

_____

_____

Execution plan: What steps will you take to get that life?

_____

_____

_____

_____

_____

Chapter 12: Key Elements

Here are the key elements covered in Chapter 12:

- Understand and practice the best technique to use when an opportunity shot presents itself.
- Approach the shot with confidence.
- See problems as challenges and challenges as opportunities.
- Know the difference between what you can and cannot control; what you can still do something about and what is over. Take the appropriate action.
- Use CORE Triumph! to make your life amazing.

Thirteen

LET'S TEE IT UP

Golf is the closest game to the game we call life. You get
bad breaks from good shots; you get good breaks from
bad shots—but you have to play the ball where it lies.

—BOBBY JONES

In this chapter, we will examine the key components and strategies to playing the game of golf and living life to your fullest potential. You were born
to do great things in life and to make a positive impact—whether it's on the
golf course, in the boardroom, at the office, or in your home. When you are
at your best, you bring out the best in others. Let's take a look now at your
CORE Triumph! plan for making the most out of every round of golf and
every day in your life.

Coaches
- Debbie O'Connell
- Debbie Crews Ketterling, PhD
- Tony Robbins

Outcome
- Play your best golf
- Be efficient and understand your intention for every shot and every day of life
- Know how to focus your attention and energy properly to Triumph

Reasons
- Enjoy playing golf even more than you do now
- Feel fabulous when you reach your goals
- Be happier every day
- Have better relationships with those around you
- Reach your full potential
- Be successful in all areas of life

Execution
- Read this chapter
- Work through this chapter
- Have an intention for each shot and day
- Eliminate thoughts and words that are negative, demeaning, or holding you back
- Replace hindering thoughts and words with language about what's possible
- Focus your attention on the goal
- Learn from the past but leave it there
- Live in the present
- Plan for and work toward all that is possible in the future

Golf is taught as a sport for life. Golf is a metaphor for life. The game challenges us with hazards, bunkers, hills, rough, and boundary lines. There are penalties. To play well, we must learn to handle the high emotions of amazing execution and success, as well as the low emotions of missed shots and lost balls. It's important to tee yourself up for success—to think and plan your next move and then follow through. And, of course, you need to keep moving in the direction of your goal. Staying in a good frame of mind makes the entire journey from tee-to-green and hole-to-hole more enjoyable and more successful.

It's time to take all of your knowledge, effort, and experience onto the golf course. Dr. Debbie Crews Ketterling is a sports psychology consultant who has researched how the brain enhances or hinders performance in the game of golf. Dr. Crews Ketterling conducted test groups with top players, as well as novice golfers, and examined the activity levels in different parts of their brains during golf activities. She has summed up over thirty years of test results in her book *Golf: Energy in Motion—It's Not About the Ball; It's About Possibilities.*

One of the key concepts in her book is intention. To put it simply, "Ask for what you want!" Dr. Crews Ketterling explains, "The body wants a set of clear and specific instructions so it can create the outcome we want." That sounds like CORE Triumph! "The system's (the brain's) job is to create what we ask for, the best that it can, at this point and time" (Crews 2005).

In order to have a clear outcome, it is very important to take the time to visualize, talk through, or feel your exact intention before you execute a shot. So if you are planning a chip-and-run shot, once you review the situation and decide on the shot and the club, be very clear about how the ball will travel. How high will it fly? Where will it land? How much will it roll? What direction will it roll? Be sure your thinking is specific and positive. Keep any self-doubt out of your thoughts. Plan and see the shot exactly as you would like to execute it.

Have you ever been in your setup and felt as if you had the wrong club in your hand? Or maybe you stood over a chip or pitch shot and made your swing only to realize afterward that you really didn't have a plan? I've experienced both of these scenarios and they usually resulted in a poor shot. If you have doubt, or you haven't thought through your intention, step away from the ball and start your pre-shot routine over. Be sure to make a clear decision and you'll have successful execution.

Although you want to clearly define your intentions be aware not to turn your intention into an expectation. According to Dr. Crews Ketterling, "Expectations are another variable that interfere with our intentions" (2006, page 31). The typical response to expectations is to try too hard by putting too much pressure on yourself. I'm sure you have experienced this both on and off the golf course. Things don't usually go as planned when you force them to happen.

Dr. Crews Ketterling banned these words from the golf course because they signal your system to try too hard to make something happen:

- Have to
- Need to
- Should
- Try

As I mentioned in Chapter 3, plan the shot exactly as you want it to happen, be specific, and ask for what you want—then get out of the way and let it happen. You may be wondering, "How do I get out of my own way?"

During a lesson, my student hit the best shot of his life on a particular swing. It felt great to him, it sounded solid, and it traveled farther and straighter than any of his other shots. We were both thrilled. On the very next swing, something happened that I've witnessed many times: he made one of his worst shots. This same thing may happen after you experience your best round on a course. I asked my student this question: "Did you try to hit that same awesome shot that you just hit?"

He smiled and said, "Yes!" I explained that you don't want to try to do what you just did; you just want to do what you did. I laughed and asked him whether I was making any sense. Basically, I was saying that just before the best swing ever, he was doing his pre-shot routine and focusing on the target. But the next swing his focused changed to copying the previous shot.

He then said it perfectly. "So, you're saying not to try to replicate the shot. Just replicate the process." I was so excited about that explanation. It's perfect! Don't try to replicate the shot. Just replicate the process!

This leads us to the next key concept from Dr. Crews Ketterling: attention. She explains, "How we focus our attention before, during and after the swing directly influences performance. How we focus our attention between shots influences our ability to focus during the shot." As we talked about in Chapter 3, the pre-shot focus is on analyzing the situation and deciding on how to execute the shot. This was referred to as the *Think Box*. From there, our focus is on the target as we set up for the shot in the *Play Box*.

Many years ago, I was playing in my first LPGA T&CP Mixed Team Tournament with a very successful PGA professional. He was a former professional baseball player who had competed in a World Series. I was very nervous and I had a hard time keeping negative thoughts and my self-doubt at bay. After all, what if I played poorly and let my partner down? I had to keep those thoughts out of my head.

My plan was to have a continuous dialogue of positive affirmations flowing in my mind for the entire round, except for the two seconds when I actually swung the club. The dialogue included such phrases as, "I am calm and confident," "I am successful and I enjoy being successful," "I have a great golf swing," and "I enjoy playing golf well."

During my pre-shot routine, I would clearly state my intention, saying something like, "I'm going to hit the ball to the shadow down the right side of the fairway." I would think the words "target" and "finish," breathe, and then be quiet and swing. As soon as I finished my swing, I would start again with positive affirmations. At the time, it was the only way that I could keep self-doubt and negative thoughts from running through my mind.

I played well! I was exhausted after talking to myself for four-and-a -half hours. It took a great amount of energy and focus to fight off the doubt. That event was the only time that I used the non-stop dialogue technique. Since then I've either been able to think positively or not think about my game. If the wrong thought pops into my head, I simply think "cancel" or "stop," and replace it with an affirming thought. This allows me to actually converse with my playing partners and look around and appreciate the beauty surrounding me, which is much more fun.

Between shots, you don't even need to think about your golf game or your confidence level. You can remove yourself from the game and have a conversation or think about something else—something positive. But if your mind goes to negative thoughts or self-doubt, you must take charge and put positive, confidence-building words into your mind.

Once you start your pre-shot routine, be in charge of your thoughts, visions, emotions, and energy. Dr. Crews Ketterling points out that you will go from a broad focus of the situation to deciding on the shot and planning the shot (intention). As you approach the ball, your focus will become narrow. What I find successful in approaching the *Play Box* is to get into my setup with a quiet mind, look at the target, and breathe in. As I look back at the ball, I breathe out and say "target" while keeping the image of my target in my mind's eye. My focus—my attention—is only on the target.

To summarize: State your intention; pay attention; and focus on what will give you optimal performance.

Live Positive!

You get what you focus on in golf and in life. A very important aspect to being successful on the golf course and in life is to let go of heavy burdens, regrets, painful experiences, and bad golf holes from your past. I often hear students comment on holes that they've never played well. Carrying around negative memories keeps you from reaching your full potential.

I was sharing a story with a friend of mine one day about a past experience that was still bothering me. He's a very wise man and he had me imagine placing that experience in a box. He said to imagine that it's with me all the time and I have to carry it everywhere so I could understand how hanging on to a negative experience could be a burden.

Do this with me: Go ahead and put your pain, guilt, or negative experience in a box, and picture yourself carrying it around. It's with you all the time, even in the shower. It gets heavier the longer you hold it. You'll find it difficult to accomplish any task as you carry this load. You can rest your arms as you sleep, but the box is still right there, on top of you, all night long.

I had this experience of actually carrying a box and it stopped me from accomplishing a task one day in the parking lot of a grocery store. My spouse and I were putting our items in the car. We removed three cases of water from the cart and then I picked up a box of six Duraflame logs we had bought for my mom and dad. When I had the heavy box in my hands, the cart started to roll away from us and down the hill. I said, "Oh, the cart!" As it rolled, I started to chase it, still carrying the box of logs. I saw a car coming out of the corner of my eye, so I was even more determined to catch the rolling cart. I actually got close enough to the cart to grab it, but my hands were full. Thankfully, the car stopped, so I stopped and watched the runaway cart pick up speed. When it hit the curb, we saw the two hot rotisserie chickens we had just purchased fly through the air as the cart flipped over. We laughed so hard! I looked at the lady in the car and she was laughing hysterically, as well.

The point of this story is that if I had not been holding the heavy box, I could have reached out and accomplished my goal. It was within my reach; I was right next to it, but the box was holding me back.

What is holding you back? What do you need to let go of in order to move forward? What is keeping you from living your best life or playing your best golf?

Even little kids have learned something about the wisdom of letting go through the popular Disney movie *Frozen* and its Oscar-winning song, *"Let It Go."*

Let it go! Let it go!
Turn away and slam the door…
It's funny how some distance
Makes everything seems small.
And the fears that once controlled me
Can't get to me at all…
The past is in the past.[41]

---

41 http://www.stlyrics.com/lyrics/frozen/letitgo.htm

This tip from Tony Robbins explains why we sometimes hold on to something from the past.

> A grudge, a feeling, a memory, an experience…these are all things we hold on to from the past. But why do we do it? We like to hold on to things, situations, and circumstances because in some weird way, it's fulfilling. There's comfort in familiarity and justification. But, holding on to the past has no real benefit—it only holds you back.
>
> …Letting go is not as hard as it may seem. Bad things happen, sure, but you cannot change the past, so why continue to perpetuate it? To let go, you have to face what has happened, accept that you can't change it, and then move on. Once you're able to move on and close old doors, inevitably new doors will open up, better opportunities will arise, and, most of all, you'll have a better story that moves you forward, instead of holding you back.[42]

Here are more awesome quotes about letting go:

- "Everybody's got a past. The past does not equal the future unless you live there" (Tony Robbins).
- "Holding on is believing that there's only a past; letting go is knowing that there's a future" (Daphne Rose Kingma).
- "Without freedom from the past, there is no freedom at all" (Jiddu Krishnamurti).
- "You've got to make a conscious choice every day to shed the old—whatever the 'old' means for you" (Sarah Ban Breathnach).

Pay attention to your thoughts and your words. Do you default to defending why you cannot Triumph? If you focus on reasons or excuses for being stuck, your brain will listen and respond appropriately. Your brain will do what you

---

42 https://www.tonyrobbins.com/mind-meaning/the-power-of-letting-go/

ask of it. You will be able to say, "See, I knew I couldn't do it!" But is that what you want, an excuse?

Stop telling your old story—which somehow makes it OK to stay stuck or even fail—and create a new story. Even when you decide to only focus on your new story and your future, negative thoughts may pop up, or you may begin to make an excuse. It's OK. You are human. Now you know to say "stop" to the chatter immediately and change the story. Every moment is a new moment. Learn from the past and move on.

I challenge you to have a day with thoughts, intentions, and words that are only about the present or future and what is possible. As you read earlier, you may not fully believe that you can direct your attention to the present or the future, but you can fully believe that it is possible. Practice every day until you have mastered this belief by thinking, intending, and saying only positive things, never once relying on the past for comfort or excuses. Move forward to Triumph!

Take a moment now to write down an experience (or possibly more than one experience) from your past that you are holding on to and that is holding you back. Is it something you can't make sense of—an abusive relationship, words that were spoken to you that have become beliefs, a broken heart, a bad experience? Or something you need to forgive yourself for? A golf hole that you haven't conquered yet? What is the story that you tell yourself to make it OK for you to not grow wings and fly?

_____

_____

_____

_____

_____

_____

Now, let's create a new story. Say out loud, "I choose to change my past negative experiences into learning events that will propel me into an amazing future!" Then, "I choose to accept what I cannot change and what I don't understand as part of life and as a part of my past. I choose to live today, each and every moment, to the fullest and look forward to tomorrow!"

Write down your new story. A story filled with possibilities, happiness, and Triumphs! Your best days are ahead!

_____

_____

_____

_____

_____

_____

Play the game of golf and the game of life with excitement and anticipation of amazing events and thrilling moments. The core of who you are is pure, positive, and happy. This doesn't mean that you won't have hazards along the way. You will. It's part of the game. The keys are to execute the best you can, learn, and move on. Life is an adventure!

This is a quote I read at my grandmother's funeral describing her life:

Life should NOT
be a journey to the grave
with the intention of arriving
safely in an attractive
and well-preserved body,
but rather to
skid in sideways,
chocolate in one hand,
martini (Seagram's 7 and club for Grandma) in the other,
body thoroughly used up, totally worn out,
and screaming,
"WOO-HOO! What a ride!"

- Maxine

Chapter 13: Key Elements

Here are the key elements covered in Chapter 13:

- Do the following for every shot on the golf course:
  - State your intention; have clarity in your shot.
  - Focus your attention on the target.
  - Let it happen.
- Let go of past negative golf holes and life experiences.
- Don't hold on to a story from your past that gives you an excuse to fail.
- Create a story of Triumph!

Fourteen

What is an extraordinary life? A life of meaning, a magnificent life, a life of joy, happiness, love, passion, success, and fulfillment. Life experienced on your terms.

—Tony Robbins

Extraordinary belongs to those who create it!

—Unknown

In this chapter, I will ask you to take an honest look at a few areas in your life. You will assess your current situation and rank it on a scale of one to ten. You will decide on an area or two in your life in which you will take immediate action to make even better. The ultimate goal is to keep you on a path in life that results in an extraordinary life. Below, find our CORE Triumph! plan for this chapter.

Coaches	Outcome	Reasons	Execution
• Debbie O'Connell	• An extraordinary life	• Why not	• Work through this chapter
• Tony Robbins	• Live the life you dream about	• Because you can	• Use this book as a reference
• John Assaraf		• To be happy	
		• You will inspire others	

An extraordinary life is one where we are living the life we envisioned for ourselves or where we are making progress toward that vision.

Many times during my career as a teacher, I've had students who are completely frustrated with their golf games. I've asked, "Does your expectation match your vision of what you want in golf as well as the effort you are putting into the game?"

I've had other students share with me that they love the game and enjoy every round, no matter how they play. I was curious why some of my students were frustrated and others were in a state of bliss.

Those who were truly having a great time playing had their expectations of the game in line with what they envisioned golf to be and in accord with the amount of effort they put into it. Someone who is a 30 handicap, but has a vision of making all pars and birdies and an expectation of competing in the championship flight for the club championship without lessons or practice, will be frustrated during every round of golf. The vision does not match reality.

But if the 30 handicap golfer has a goal of being a single-digit handicap and competing for the club championship, works through CORE Triumph!, and executes the plan, their progress will be exciting. By executing the plan with energy, they can meet their goal.

Let's take some time to examine different areas of your life. After all, an extraordinary life contains more than just golf. We are going to examine our golf, physical health, relationships, finances, career, spirituality, and contributions to society. To live an extraordinary life, it's important to continue to learn, grow, and show progress in all of these areas. Of course, you cannot have precise focus and all-out effort in all categories at all times, so let's first take an honest look at where you rank yourself in each area now. Then, you will choose one or two areas on which to focus your effort and energy.

In the chart below, rank your assessment of your current situation in these areas of your life at this moment, with 10 being the highest. Rankings will be quite individual, meaning a 10 in finances for one person may be to live debt free and be able to vacation for a month. Another person may deem a 10 in finances as being a billionaire, owning a jet, a yacht, and four homes. Be completely honest with yourself. Color in the column from the bottom up to where you rank your life in each category. The ultimate goal is to fill in the entire base of the Trophy of Triumph!.

	Golf	Health Physical Body	Relationships	Finances	Career	Spirituality	Contributions
10							
8							
6							
4							
2							
0							

Take a few minutes to think about each category and write down what a 10 would look like for you. Don't worry about how you'll get to the 10—just brainstorm about what it means to you to color in the entire column for each category of the Trophy of Triumph. Dream big!

Golf:

_____

_____

_____

_____

Physical health:

_____

_____

_____

_____

Relationships:

_____

_____

_____

_____

Finances:

_____

_____

_____

_____

Career:

_____

_____

_____
_____

Spirituality:

_____
_____
_____
_____

Contributions:

_____
_____
_____
_____

Now, choose one or two areas where you are going to put your focus and effort for the next 30 days. My suggestion is to start with your physical body if your current ranking is below a 6. The reason for this suggestion is because you will feel better and have more energy, which will make all of the other categories better as well.

1. First focus area: _____
Coach(es):

_____

Outcome:

_____
_____

Reasons:

_____
_____
_____

Execution:

_____

_____

_____

_____

2. Second focus area: _____

Coach(es):

_____

Outcome:

_____

_____

Reasons:

_____

_____

_____

Execution:

_____

_____

_____

Remember the "tri" in Triumph! is to remind you to continually analyze your progress and adjust your execution plan when needed. Finally, plan your celebrations!

Thirty days after starting, fill out this chart. Date: _____

Sixty days after starting, fill out this chart again. Date: _____

Ninety days after starting, fill out this chart again. Date: _____

One year after starting, fill out this chart again. Date: _____

Here are some additional proven ways to reach your ideal outcome and live an extraordinary life:

1. Watch your language. Change your words and you will take charge of your life.

Disempowering Words	Empowering Words
Disgusted	Surprised
Exhausted or tired	Recharging
Afraid	Curious
I hate	I prefer
Terrible	Different
Anxious	Eager
Problem	Challenge
Picky	Loves quality
Weird	Unique
Overwhelmed	In demand
Nervous	Excited
Failed	Learned something
Confused	About to learn
Stressed	Striving or blessed
Challenges	Opportunities
I have to	I choose to or I get to

Average Words	Energizing Words
Awake	Energized
Good	Extraordinary
Happy	Elated
Nice	Marvelous
Pretty	Beautiful
Smart	Brilliant
Quick	Explosive
Growing	Flourishing
Neat	Immaculate

2. Make a vision board of what you want your life to be. Use pictures as a representation of what you want to achieve. On your board, glue a picture of a scorecard, pictures of family fun and vacations, and images of the types of relationships you want to have, the house you want, the car you'll drive, the check you will give to charity—everything you want and plan to attain. Look at this vision board every day for three to five minutes. Feel the emotions of success and an extraordinary life.

3. Use meditation and visualization to see and feel the positive emotions of your future. As I learned from John Assaraf, connecting visual images with emotions and goals will create patterns in your brain that will go deep into your subconscious. He calls this "priming your brain for success."[43] Your brain will then be conditioned to be comfortable with this lifestyle. It will also focus on and see everything around you that supports your vision. Your beliefs and habits will help you to think about, feel, and live the life that you want to live—your extraordinary life.

Use CORE Triumph! to achieve all you want in life. You can do it! You can be who you want to be! You can live the life of your dreams!

Be Positive! Golf Positive! Live Positive!

Visit GolfPositive.com for more information and to view video lessons.

---

43 http://m.huffpost.com/us/entry/1179424

My Gift to You!

Congratulations on completing Golf Positive! Live Positive! I hope you enjoyed it! More importantly, I hope it will make a positive and significant difference in your life.

My vision and mission is to make a positive and powerful impact on the world. I want to empower and educate as many people as possible on how to live a happy fulfilling life. It's a calling I have felt deep inside since I was a teenager. You are now part of my mission! Let's change the world together.

If you believe you are ready to take the lessons revealed in this book to a deeper level, I encourage you to accept a very special gift I want to give you.

I will share the five must have techniques to live triumphantly! Join me in my free one hour video workshop at LivePositiveGift.com. Make your life even better!

See you soon!
Debbie

Glossary of Golf Terms

address: When a golfer takes their stance and lines up the club to make a stroke.

apron: The short fringe surrounding the green where the grass is cut slightly higher than the green surface but shorter than the surrounding rough. (see *collar* or *fringe*)

backswing: When the golfer moves the club backward away from the addressed ball in preparation for the forward movement of the swing.

ball mark: The mark left by the ball when it lands on the fairway or green.

birdie: One under par for the hole.

bogey: One over par for the hole.

bunker: Shallow pits filled with sand and generally incorporating a raised lip or barrier, from which the ball is more difficult to play than from grass. Can be located anywhere on the course (greenside bunker, fairway bunker).

caddie: A person who carries a player's clubs, assists a player on deciding distances and club selection and helps the player when deciding on the line of a putt.

clubface: The part of the clubhead that comes into direct contact with the ball

clubhead: The part of the golf club attached to the end of the shaft that is built for striking the golf ball.

collar: The short fringe surrounding the green where the grass is cut slightly higher than the green surface, but shorter that the surrounding rough. (see *apron* or *fringe*)

divot: A piece of turf lifted when ball is struck.

dogleg: A hole where the fairway turns to the left or right.

downhill lie: When the ball rests on a hill that goes down toward where you intend to strike the ball.

downswing: The downstroke part of a golfer's swing.

draw: As the ball travels in the air, it curves from the player's right to the player's left (for the right-handed golfer) and from the player's left to the player's right (for the left-handed golfer). Opposite of a fade.

drive: A shot from the teeing area.

driving range: An area constructed for practice. Most driving ranges have targets.

fade: As the ball travels in the air, it curves from the player's left to the player's right (for the right-handed golfer) and from the player's right to the player's left (for the left-handed golfer). Opposite of a draw.

fringe: Refers to any grass adjoining the putting surface that is mowed to a height only slightly higher than the grass on the green, a height typically about halfway between green and fairway heights. Fringe can be used a synonym for either apron or collar, but is most commonly used in the sense of collar.

golf club, parts of *(see clubface, clubhead, heel hosel, shaft, toe)*

green: The green, or putting green, is the culmination of a golf hole, where the flagstick and hole are located. Getting the golf ball into the hole on the putting green is the object of the game of golf. Greens can vary widely in shape and size, but are most commonly oval or oblong in shape.

heel: The part of the clubhead nearest the hosel.

hook: A hook shot is normally a badly hit ball that curves hard left for the right-handed golfer, opposite the slice.

hosel: A socket in the clubhead into which the shaft is inserted.

lead side: See *target side*.

par: The number of strokes an expert golfer is expected to need to complete an individual hole or all the holes on a golf course. The value assigned to represent par for an individual hole is always comprised of two putts and the number of strokes it should take to reach the green. For beginners, it gives you an idea of the length of the hole. The shortest holes are typically par-3; par-4 is medium length; and the longest holes on a golf course are usually par-5.

pull side of the target: Left of the target for a right-handed golfer and right of the target for a left-handed golfer.

push side of the target: Right of the target for a right-handed golfer and left of the target for a left-handed golfer.

putting green: See *green*.

set up: A golfer is in position and ready to play a stroke.

shaft: The long, tapered tube that connects the golfer's hands to the clubhead.

slice: A *sliced* shot is a shot that curves hard right for the right-handed golfer, opposite of the *hook*.

target line: An imaginary straight line from the intended target back to the ball.

target side: The side of the player's body nearest to the target at address (left side for the right-handed golfer and the right side for the left-handed golfer).

toe: The part of the clubhead farthest from the hosel.

trail side: The side of the player's body farthest from the target at address (right side for the right-handed golfer and the left side for the left-handed golfer).

Selected Bibliography

Amabile, Teresa and Steven J. Kramer. "The Power of Small Wins." *Harvard Business Review*, May 2011. https://hbr.org/2011/05/the-power-of-small-wins.

Crews, PhD, Debbie. *Golf: Energy in Motion—It's Not About the Ball; It's About the Possibilities* (City: Publisher, 2006).

Enhanger, Kjell, and Samantha Wallace. *Quantum Golf: The Path to Golf Mastery* (New York: Warner Books, 1991).

Gable, Shelly L., Gian C. Gonzaga, and Amy Strachman. "Will You Be There for Me When Things Go Right? Supportive Responses to Positive Event Disclosures." *Journal of Personality and Social Psychology*, 91 (2006): 904–917. http://dx.doi.org/10.1037/0022-3514.91.5.904.

Nilsson, Pia, and Lynn Marriott. *Every Shot Must Have A Purpose*. New York: Penguin Group, 2005.

Owen, David. "My Tech: Sleep Better, Play Better." *Golf Digest*. April 29, 2012. http://www.golfdigest.com/story/david-owen-tech-2012-06.

Wynne, Clive D. L., PhD, and Monique A. R. Udell, PhD. *Animal Cognition: Evolution, Behavior and Cognition*. New York: Palgrave Macmillan, 2013.

59282360R00098

Made in the USA
Columbia, SC
03 June 2019